Law School Survival Guide

Constitutional Criminal Procedure

Outlines and Case Summaries

t TellerBooks

CONSTITUTIONAL
CRIMINAL PROCEDURE:
Outlines and Case Studies™

Law School Survival Guides

Published by JURALAW™
an imprint of TELLERBOOKS™

tellerbooks.com/juralaw
contact@tellerbooks.com

© 2007-12 by TellerBooks™. All rights reserved. No part of this publication may be reproduced or transmitted in any form or by any means, including photocopying, recording, or copying to any storage and retrieval system.

ISBN (13): 978-1-300-10580-0
ISBN (10): 1-300-10580-0

2012 Edition
Manufactured in the U.S.A.

DISCLAIMER: Although this book is designed to provide rigorously researched information, it is intended not as a definitive statement of the law, but rather, as a concise and general overview that will help readers to understand basic legal principles and find further information, if necessary. Because the law changes rapidly through new statutes and innovative judicial decisions, law books, including this one, may quickly become outdated. Furthermore, some decisions may be ambiguous and subject to differing interpretations and other sources may come to conclusions distinct from those presented herein. Nothing in this book forms an attorney-client relationship or is intended to constitute legal advice, which should be obtained through consultation with a qualified attorney.

SUMMARY CONTENTS

Detailed Contents		**5**
Abbreviations		**8**
1	The Exclusionary Rule in Searches and Seizures	10
2	Obtaining, Challenging, and Executing Search Warrants	16
3	Exceptions to the Invalidity of Warrantless Searches and Seizures	19
4	The Fifth Amendment Double Jeopardy Clause	27
5	The Fifth Amendment Self-Incrimination Clause	33
6	Fifth Amendment Grand Juries, Due Process, and Charging	43
7	Sixth Amendment Trial Rights	45
8	The Sixth Amendment Confrontation Clause	52
9	The Sixth Amendment Right to Counsel	56
Review Charts and Summaries		64
Table of Cases		**67**
Thematic Index		**70**

Look for all of these titles in the

TellerBooks

Law School Survival Guides Series

(Outlines and Case Summaries)*:

TORTS

PROPERTY

CIVIL PROCEDURE

INTERNATIONAL LAW

CONTRACTS AND SALES

CONST. CRIMINAL PROCEDURE

BUSINESS ORGANIZATIONS

CONSTITUTIONAL LAW

CRIMINAL LAW

FAMILY LAW

EVIDENCE

*Available in paperback,
iPhone, Kindle,
Nook and pdf formats.

Visit us at TellerBooks.com/studyguides

DETAILED CONTENTS

Summary Contents		3
Detailed Contents		5
Abbreviations		8
1	**The Exclusionary Rule in Searches and Seizures**	**10**
1.1	Individual Rights under the Constitution	10
1.2	The Exclusionary Rule and Other Remedies	10
1.3	Limitations on the Exclusionary Rule	11
1.4	Technological Surveillance	12
1.5	"Fruit of the Poisonous Tree" and Purging the Taint	12
1.6	The Exclusionary Rule Applied to Fifth Amendment Violations	13
1.7	Standing and Scope of the Fourth Amendment	13
1.8	Curtilage	14
1.9	Arrest	14
2	**Obtaining, Challenging, and Executing Search Warrants**	**16**
2.1	Introduction	16
2.2	The Requirements of a Valid Warrant	16
2.3	Probable Cause with Respect to Anonymous Informants	17
2.4	Challenging the Warrant: the Four Corners Rule	18
2.5	Executing the Warrant	18
3	**Exceptions to the Invalidity of Warrantless Searches and Seizures**	**19**
3.2	Search Incident to Lawful Arrest	19
3.3	The Carroll Doctrine/Automobile Exception	20
3.4	Hot Pursuit	21
3.5	The Emergency Doctrine	21
3.6	Exigent Circumstances	22
3.7	Plain View Exception	23
3.8	Frisk after Terry Stop	24
3.9	Consent	25
3.10	Regulatory Searches	26
3.11	Special Needs Situations	26
3.12	Community Caretaker/Inventory Search	26
3.13	Search and Seizure Analysis Sumary	27
4	**The Fifth Amendment Double Jeopardy Clause**	**27**
4.1	Introduction	27
4.2	When Jeopardy Attaches	28
4.3	When Jeopardy Applies	28

4.4	Special Contexts	28
4.5	Collateral Estoppel and Double Jeopardy	29
4.6	Dual Sovereignty Doctrine	31
4.7	Appeals	32
4.8	Retroactivity	33

5 The Fifth Amendment Self-Incrimination Clause — 33

5.1	Overview of The Privilege	33
5.2	The *Miranda* Safeguards	35
5.3	The Two-Prong Threshold Test	36
5.4	Custody and Interrogation	36
5.5	The Exclusionary Remedy	38
5.6	Public Safety Exception to Exclusion	39
5.7	Purging an Illegal Confession Through a Repeat Confession	40
5.8	The "Fruit of the Poisonous Tree" within the *Miranda* Context	40
5.9	The Right to Counsel in Interrogations	40
5.10	The Requirement to Testify if Offered Immunity	41
5.11	Invocation and Waiver of the *Miranda* Rights	41

6 Fifth Amendment Grand Juries, Due Process, and Charging — 43

6.1	Grand Jury Indictments	43
6.2	Charging, Due Process and Equal Protection	44

7 Sixth Amendment Trial Rights — 45

7.1	Introduction to the Sixth Amendment	45
7.2	The Right to a Speedy Trial	45
7.3	The Right to a Fair Trial, the Press, and Publicity	46
7.4	The Right to a Trial by an Impartial Jury	48
7.5	The Right to a Fair Trial: Jury Selection	49
7.6	The Right to a Fair Trial: Exculpatory Evidence	50
7.7	The Right to a Fair Trial: an Impartial Judge	51

8 The Sixth Amendment Confrontation Clause — 52

8.1	The Incidental Rights to Be Present and Informed of the Accusation	52
8.2	Introduction to the Confrontation Clause	53
8.3	The History of the Confrontation Clause	53
8.4	The Confrontation Clause Today	54
8.5	Limitations	55

9 The Sixth Amendment Right to Counsel — 56

9.1	Introduction	56
9.2	When the Right to Counsel Attaches	56
9.3	The Right to Counsel During Identifications	57
9.4	Restriction on Right to Retained Counsel	59
9.5	Right to Counsel on Appeal	59
9.6	Right to Experts	60
9.7	Effective Assistance of Counsel	61
9.8	Conflicts of Interest in Multiple Representation	62
9.9	Self-Representation	63

Review Charts and Summaries **64**

When Constitutional Rights Apply 64
Landmark Criminal Procedure Cases 64

Table of Cases **67**

Thematic Index **70**

ABBREVIATIONS

A	Grantee (for present estate/future interest hypotheticals)
AGI	Adjusted gross income
AP	Adverse possession
A/R	Assumption of the risk
B	Buyer
BFP	Bona fide purchaser or bona fide purchase
C	Constitution
CIF	Cause-in-fact
Cl.	Clause
CLEO	State Chief Law Enforcement Officer
Court (cap.)	United States Supreme Court
CP	Court of Pleas (UK)
CR	Contingent remainder
CSD	Common Scheme of Development
CSI	Compelling state interest
Ct.	Court
Ct. App.	Court of Appeals
Ct. Chan.	Court of Chancery (England)
ED	Emotional distress
EI	Executory interest
Eng.	England
ES	Equitable Servitude
FI	false imprisonment
FLSA	Fair Labor Standards Act
FMLA	Family and Medical Leave Act
FQJ	Federal question jurisdiction
FRAP	Federal Rules of Appellate Procedure
FRCP	Federal Rules of Civil Procedure
FRCrP	Federal Rules of Criminal Procedure
FRE	Federal Rules of Evidence
FS	Fee simple absolute (fee simple)
FSCS	Fee simple on condition subsequent
FSD	Fee simple determinable
FS EL	Fee simple on executory limitation
FT	Fee tail
H.L.	House of Lords (England)
IIED	Intentional infliction of emotional distress
IT	Intentional tort
JMOL	Judgment as a matter of law
JNOV	Judgment non obstante veredicto
J/SL	Joint and several liability, or jointly and severally liable
JT	Joint tenant/tenancy
K	Knowledge (criminal law) or Contract (all other law)
K.B.	King's Bench (UK)
KSC	Knowledge to a substantial certainty
L	Loss in value
L1	First landlord
Lat.	Latin
LE	Life estate
LED	Life estate determinable
LLC	Limited liability company
LLP	Limited liability partnership
LRM	Least restrictive means
MPC	Model Penal Code
MSAJ	Motion to set aside the judgment
N	Negligence
N.B.	Nota bene
NIED	Negligent infliction of emotional distress
O	Original owner, or grantor (in present estates and future interests)
OLQ	Owner of the *locus in quo*

OO	Original owner
P	Purpose or purchaser
PJ	Personal jurisdiction
PJI	Pattern Criminal Jury Instruction
Q.B.	Queen's Bench (UK)
R	Recklessness
RAP	Rule against perpetuities
RC	Real Covenant
Restatement	Restatement (of Contracts, Torts, Judgments, etc.)
RFRA	Religious Freedom Restoration Act of 1993
RIL	Res ipsa loquitur
RPP	Reasonable prudent person
Rule	Federal Rule of Evidence or Federal Rule of Civil Procedure
§	Section
S	Sublessee or seller
S.Ct.	Supreme Court or U.S. Supreme Court Reporter
SJ	Summary judgment
SL	Strict liability
SMJ	Subject matter jurisdiction
SP	Specific performance
T1	First tenant
TE	Tenant/tenancy by the entireties
TO	True owner
UCC	Uniform Commercial Code
US	United States of America or United States Reports (compilation of U.S. Supreme Court opinions)
USC	United States Code
VR	Vested remainder
VR SD	Vested remainder subject to divestment

1 The Exclusionary Rule in Searches and Seizures

1.1 Individual Rights under the Constitution

1.1.1 Many of the founders did not support enumerating individual rights in the Constitution.

1.1.2 Many of them, including James Madison, the Constitution's principal author, instead supported enumerating rights in state constitutions.

1.1.3 The Bill of Rights was nonetheless included for political reasons. However, it originally applied only to the federal government—*not* to the states.

1.1.4 This was changed under the Fourteenth Amendment, which has in large part incorporated the Bill of Rights. Today, the following criminal procedural provisions have been incorporated:

  (a) **Fourth Amendment**: protection against illegal searches and seizures;

  (b) **Fifth Amendment**: right against self-incrimination; due process under the law; protection against double jeopardy;

  (c) **Sixth Amendment**: confrontation of witnesses; the right to counsel;

  (d) **Eighth Amendment**: right to be free of cruel or unusual punishment.

1.1.5 However, certain constitutional guarantees in federal court do not apply to the states, including:

  (a) The right to a grand jury indictment for felonies (Fifth Amendment);

  (b) The right to a jury trial in all criminal cases (Seventh Amendment).

1.2 The Exclusionary Rule and Other Remedies

1.2.1 The exclusionary rule requires a court to exclude evidence obtained in violation of the Constitution. *Boyd v. United States* (U.S. 1886) (the landmark exclusionary rule case).

1.2.2 The courts have long struggled with what to do with the excluded evidence. One potential solution was to return it to the defendant.

  (a) *See Weeks v. United States* (U.S. 1914) (William Day, J.), where letters were seized unlawfully without a warrant. Held: in order to prevent the government from using the evidence on retrial, it should be returned.

  (b) *N.B.*: this court's overbroad holding failed to take into account situations when the government seized drugs and other contraband.

1.2.3 Parties have tried to get around *Weeks* in various ways.

  (a) *See Silverthorn Lumber Co. v. United States* (U.S. 1920) (Holmes, J.), where the plaintiff seized the defendant Silverthorn Lumber Co.'s originals, photocopied them, and returned them. Held:

this act violates the intent of *Weeks*. The exclusionary rule applies not only to the original evidence, but also to the fruits (or in this case, copies) of the evidence.

1.2.4 Twenty nine years later, the Fourth Amendment was incorporated against the states in *Wolf v. People of the State of Colorado* (U.S. 1949) (Frankfurter, J.), since it was comprised of rights "implicit in the concept of ordered liberty."

1.2.5 However, the **exclusionary rule** was not incorporated against the states until *Mapp v. Ohio* (U.S. 1961) (Clark, J.), where police entered the defendant's home without a search warrant and found obscene materials that they used to convict her. Thus, in 1961 there came a bright line rule: the Fourth Amendment applied to the states through the Fourteenth Amendment. From that moment onward, if state law enforcement violated the defendant's constitutional rights, the judicially created exclusionary applied as a sanction, just as it would had the violation been at the hands of federal law enforcement.

1.3 Limitations on the Exclusionary Rule

1.3.1 The exclusionary rule does *not exclude all illegally obtained* evidence *for all purposes*.

1.3.2 Such illegally obtained evidence may be used, for example, to impeach the defendant if he testifies contrary to the excluded evidence.

1.3.3 The exclusionary rule applies to the person on trial, but if someone else's constitutional rights have been violated, the person on trial has no standing to exclude it.

1.3.4 In recent years, the Court has been limiting the scope of the exclusionary rule, holding that it acts to exclude evidence obtained *through* **police misconduct only**, not through the errors of others (*e.g.*, a magistrate who erroneously grants a warrant). *U.S. v. Leon* (U.S. 1984) (White, J.).

    (a) Rationale: excluding evidence *when another party errs* will not have a deterrent effect on the police. *U.S. v. Leon* (U.S. 1984) (White, J.).

    (b) The *"good faith" exception* to the exclusionary rule allows evidence to be admitted when police, acting with good faith, reasonably rely on the validity of a warrant, even if the warrant is invalid.

1.3.5 The Fourth Amendment is designed to protect citizens from illegal government searches. Thus, information obtained by a **search conducted by a private or corporate person is admissible** and does not need to be excluded when used by the government for prosecution (unless the person conducting the search is an agent of the government).

    (a) *See Jacobsen*, where the Drug Enforcement Agency was permitted to use evidence obtained from FedEx, which broke open packages to be mailed, discovered cocaine, and turned them over to the government.

1.3.6 Traditionally, grand juries have been able to function without all of the same limits as those placed in trials.

    (a) In *United States v. Calandra* (U.S. 1974) (Powell, J.), the Court limited the application of the exclusionary rule so as not to "seriously impede the grand jury."

    (b) Illegally obtained evidence is thus admissible in grand jury proceedings.

1.3.7 The exclusionary rule applies only to criminal cases. In civil cases, the exclusionary rule does not apply because no liberty interest is jeopardized.

1.4 Technological Surveillance

1.4.1 Searches from the outside of a person's home using **technological devices that are outside of ordinary public use** are presumed to be unreasonable searches requiring a warrant under the Fourth Amendment.

   (a) *See Kyllo v. United States* (U.S. 2001) (Scalia, J.), where the Court excluded evidence obtained with a thermal imaging device from a helicopter that showed that the defendant had been using heat lamps for growing marijuana plants in his home. Because the apparatus was not within the ordinary public use, the defendant had a reasonable expectation of privacy that was violated.

1.4.2 This rule does not extend to drug-sniffing canines.

   (a) *See Illinois v. Caballes* (U.S. 2005) (Stevens, J.), where a narcotics dog sniffed drugs in the trunk of the defendant, who was stopped by a trooper. The defendant argued that just as evidence obtained with the heat imaging device was excluded, so too should the drugs be excluded. Held: the analogy cannot be drawn. Here, the only information that could be obtained is incriminating. A heat imaging device could, on the other hand, invade legitimate privacy rights, such as the hour that a resident enters her sauna.

1.5 "Fruit of the Poisonous Tree" and Purging the Taint

1.5.1 When police effect an illegal search or seizure, both illegally obtained primary evidence as well as all derivative evidence, including verbal statements, is to be excluded at trial as *"tainted fruit of the poisonous tree." Wong Sun v. United States* (U.S. 1963) (Brennan, J.).

1.5.2 However, the taint may be **purged** through the following:

   (a) Inevitable Discovery

      (i) If police can show that the evidence was to be inevitably discovered, it is admissible in trial.

      (ii) *See Nix v. Williams* (U.S. 1984) (Warren Burger, C.J.), where a suspect was arrested by police when a ten year old girl went missing. In order to elicit an incriminating response from the defendant, a police officer said to another officer in the presence of the defendant that the least he could do is offer the girl's family a "Christian burial." The defendant then led the officers to the body of the victim, thus incriminating himself. However, although the defendant's constitutional rights were violated, the evidence was not excluded, since it was going to be inevitably discovered by independent sources in a matter of time.

   (b) Intervening Voluntary Conduct

      (i) Intervening voluntary conduct, such as a voluntary, subsequent confession by the defendant, purges the tainted fruit of the poisonous tree.

(ii) *See Wong Sun v. United States* (U.S. 1963) (Brennan, J.), where an unlawful arrest resulted in both a confession (primary evidence) and a witness lead (derivative evidence). The Court excluded both. Held: since the heroin would not have been seized but for the unlawful questioning of Toy, it is excluded. However, Sun's testimony is admissible because it has no connection to the arrest. Rather, it was voluntarily made.

1.6 The Exclusionary Rule Applied to Fifth Amendment Violations

1.6.1 If a party is unlawfully arrested or detained, the testimony obtained is **automatically inadmissible** if the party's *Miranda* rights are not read.

1.6.2 Yet reading the *Miranda* rights on its own is not sufficient to make the confession admissible.

1.6.3 Under *Brown v. Illinois* (U.S. 1975) (Blackmun, J.), the following factors are to be considered when determining whether the confession is admissible:

(a) The *presence of intervening events*;

(b) The *flagrancy of the police misconduct*; and

(c) The *amount of time elapsed* between the illegal act and the confession.

(i) Six hours is too little time to purge the taint of the confession. *Taylor v. Alabama* (U.S. 1982) (Marshall, J.).

1.6.4 The Court affirmed *Brown v. Illinois* in *Dunaway v. New York* (U.S. 1979) (Brennan, J.). Because the confession could not be separated from the initial illegality, it was excluded.

1.7 Standing and Scope of the Fourth Amendment

1.7.1 Traditional Rule: Standing Requires a Possessory Interest

(a) In *Olmstead v. United States* (U.S. 1928) (Taft, C.J.), the Court held that the Fourth Amendment did not apply to a *wiretap* on a telephone pole outside of the defendant's home, since the defendant **did not have a possessory interest** in the pole and conversations were not protected by the Fourth Amendment.

(b) Under the law as it existed shortly after WWII, the only way to make a motion to exclude evidence would be to admit ownership.

(c) This led to problems when the evidence was contraband. If the defendant admitted ownership, he would incriminate himself; but if he did not admit ownership, he would lack standing to challenge admission of the evidence.

(d) Thus, in *Jones v. United States* (U.S. 1960) (Frankfurter, J.), the Court resolved this problem by granting defendants **automatic standing**. Without needing to admit ownership of contraband, defendants could challenge the admission of such contraband into evidence.

1.7.2 Modern Rule: Standing Requires a Reasonable Expectation of Privacy

(a) *Olmstead* (U.S. 1928) was later overruled, with a new rule pronounced in *Katz v. United States* (U.S. 1967) (Stewart, J.). Even if a defendant lacks a proprietary interest in a telephone booth, a wiretap infringes on a **reasonable expectation of privacy** that therefore requires that police obtain a search warrant.

- (b) The reasonable expectation of privacy standard involves a two-prong test:

    - (i) Does the defendant assert a **subjective interest** in privacy?

    - (ii) If so, is **society prepared to accept** that subjective privacy expectation as an area that is private?

- (c) *Rakas v. Illinois* (U.S. 1978) (Rehnquist, J.) modified *Jones*, holding that the *Jones* "legitimately on premises" test was overbroad. Just because the defendant is legitimately on the premises does not mean that he has standing to challenge the search or seizure.

    - (i) The new test is whether the defendant has a **reasonable expectation of privacy** based on *Katz v. United States* (U.S. 1967). The defendant **has the burden of establishing both prongs.**

    - (ii) *The defendant* has standing to challenge evidence if he owns or has a right to possess the place or thing searched. A car passenger therefore has no standing to challenge a search of that car.

- (d) Because Fourth Amendment rights are personal, a party may not demand that evidence be excluded when that party was not the direct victim of a constitutional violation. *United States v. Payner* (U.S. 1980).

- (e) Ownership of items on its own does not give rise to standing to challenge a Fourth Amendment search or seizure.

    - (i) See *Rawlings v. Kentucky* (U.S. 1980) (Rehnquist), where the court did not apply the exclusionary rule against drugs seized from the defendant's companion's purse, because the defendant did not have a **reasonable expectation of privacy** in the purse.

1.8 Curtilage

1.8.1 Individuals have a reasonable expectation of privacy in their homes.

1.8.2 This privacy expectation encompasses the curtilage—the *dwelling* and *all buildings and property immediately surrounding it*. *Oliver v. United States* (U.S. 1984).

1.8.3 The privacy expectation does *not extend to distant fields* on the property. *Hester v. United States* (U.S. 1924).

1.8.4 The government must therefore have a warrant to search the dwelling and the curtilage, but not to the distant property outside of the curtilage. *Oliver v. United States* (U.S. 1984).

1.9 Arrest

1.9.1 Defining an Arrest

- (a) An arrest occurs when a person is taken into custody for the purpose of a criminal action. *Dunaway v. New York* (U.S. 1979).

(b) Under *Henry v. United States* (U.S. 1959) (Douglas, J.), it is more precisely the **restriction of movement** of citizens by the police.

(c) In *California v. Hodari D.* (U.S. 1991) (Scalia, J.), the Court modified the definition pronounced in *Henry*: one is arrested if his movement is restricted when he: (i) is *touched*; (ii) is taken into the *physical custody* of the officer; or (iii) *submits to the authority* of the officer.

    (i) See *California v. Hodari D.* (U.S. 1991), where a youth took note of police officers, panicked, and fled and the officers chased after him. While he was fleeing, the youth threw down a rock of crack cocaine, which was later seized by an officer. The defendant moved to suppress the crack cocaine as an illegal seizure. Held on *certiorari*: the defendant was not arrested at the time he fled and by extension, at the time the officer found the crack cocaine. Therefore, there was no illegal seizure. Judgment reversed.

1.9.2 Constitutional Requirements

(a) The Fourth Amendment requires that searches and seizures must be reasonable. An arrest, which is a "seizure" of a person, must fall into one of the following categories to be reasonable:

    (i) Made with an **arrest warrant** (which is based on probable cause); or

    (ii) Based on **probable cause** to arrest.

        (1) This is determined based on an **objective standard.**

        (2) See *Maryland v. Pringle* (U.S. 2003) (Rehnquist), where police stopped a car for speeding and received consent to search it and found cocaine. The lower court ruled that the defendant's being a front seat passenger of the car that held the cocaine was *insufficient probable cause to warrant an arrest*. On appeal, the Supreme Court (Rehnquist, J.) held that probable cause equates **reasonable grounds** *to believe someone is guilty*. In this case, there is sufficient probable cause that *someone* committed a crime.

1.9.3 Arrest Warrants

(a) Absent *exigent circumstances*, police must have a warrant to enter a defendant's home to arrest him. *Payton v. New York* (U.S. 1980) (Stevens, J.).

(b) Once an arrest warrant is issued, police have the implicit right to enter into the defendant's home to search for him.

(c) However, police with an arrest warrant do not have the implicit right to enter into the home of **third parties** to search for the defendant identified on the warrant. *Steagald v. United States* (U.S. 1981) (Marshall).

(d) Arrest warrants are *not required for felonies*.

2 Obtaining, Challenging, and Executing Search Warrants

2.1 Introduction

2.1.1 This section deals specifically with search warrants.

2.1.2 However, many of the requirements parallel those that apply to arrest warrants, which require:

    (a)   Probable cause;

    (b)   Support by oath or affirmation;

    (c)   A description with particularity of the person to be arrested; and

    (d)   Issuance by a neutral and detached magistrate.

2.1.3 Many of the rules articuled below are applicable to arrest warrants by analogy.

2.2 The Requirements of a Valid Warrant

2.2.1 Probable Cause

    (a)   Probable cause exists if, based on the facts presented to the magistrate, a reasonable person would conclude that *more likely than not*, contraband or other evidence will be at the place to be searched **at the time the warrant is executed.**

    (b)   This may be at a **future time;** anticipatory warrants are constitutional.

        (i)   *See United States v. Grubbs* (U.S. 2006) (Scalia, J.), where a magistrate issued an anticipatory warrant to police who sought to intercept child pornography at a future delivery that, according to their sources, was to occur. The defendant moved to suppress because no crime was in progress when the warrant was issued. The Court held that probable cause may exist when evidence shows that a crime **will take place**.

    (c)   However, probable cause dissipates when the facts presented to the magistrate are **too remote in time.**

2.2.2 Supported by Oath or Affirmation

    (a)   The Fourth Amendment requires the warrant to be "supported by Oath or affirmation."

2.2.3 Particularity

    (a)   The warrant must describe *with specificity* the place to be searched and the persons or things to be seized.

    (b)   *See Groh v. Ramirez* (U.S. 2004) (Stevens, J.), where the Fourth Amendment was violated because the affidavit and warrant stated with particularity only what was to be searched, not what was to be seized.

2.2.4 A Neutral and Detached Magistrate

(a) A **search warrant** must be issued by a neutral and detached magistrate.

(b) A justice of the peace who is a state attorney would not qualify.

    (i) See *Coolidge v. New Hampshire* (U.S. 1971) (Potter, J.), where a search warrant issued by a prosecutor failed because it was issued not by a neutral and detached magistrate of the Judicial Branch, but rather, by an Executive Branch official.

(c) The warrant itself must give a particular description of the things to be seized. The description may not be granted *after* the things are seized.

    (i) See *Lo-Ji Sales Inc. v. New York* (U.S. 1979) (Burger, C.J.), where a warrant describing obscene materials *after they were seized* from an adult bookstore was deemed invalid.

2.3 Probable Cause with Respect to Anonymous Informants

2.3.1 An anonymous informant is known by the police, but not by the magistrate or the defense.

2.3.2 In the earlier days of the Court, no fixed rule was given on whether the identity of anonymous informants used in police affidavits needed to be revealed.

(a) In *Roviaro v. United States* (U.S. 1957) (Burton, J.), the defendant was convicted for possessing and transporting heroine across state lines. When the defendant attacked the evidence of an anonymous informant who he wanted disclosed, the Court applied a balancing test between the defendant's need of the information for his defense and the plaintiff's desire to protect the health, welfare, and safety of the informant.

2.3.3 In *Aguilar v. Texas* (U.S. 1964) (Goldberg, J.), the Court required magistrates to apply the following two-prong test on affidavits before issuing warrants:

(a) The Basis of Knowledge Prong

    (i) There must be sufficient information showing how the informant arrived at his conclusions.

    (ii) The magistrate may consider, for example, whether the informant was an eyewitness or whether his source is hearsay.

(b) The Veracity Prong

    (i) Sufficient indicia must establish the informant's reliability. An undercover police officer, for example, would pass.

    (ii) The affiant should also include whether the anonymous informant had been used in the past and if so, whether he was reliable.

2.3.4 Later, the **Aguilar-Spinelli test** was developed.

(a) In *Spinelli v. United States* (U.S. 1969), Justice Harlan fleshed out the first prong, resulting in the *Aguilar-Spinelli* test, applying *only to anonymous informants*.

(b) According to this test, insufficient knowledge on the part of the informant may be overcome if the informant gives *enough detail to show that he is not just engaging in gossip.*

2.3.5 This test was followed until 1983, when the much laxer **totality of the circumstances** standard was established by the Supreme Court.

    (a) In *Illinois v. Gates* (U.S. 1983) (Rehnquist, C.J.), the Court held that probable cause should not be based on the two-prong test, but rather, on what a person's **common sense would dictate to be probable cause** (a "more likely than not" reasonable basis for belief) based on the totality of the circumstances. Corroboration from other sources and the informant's reliability are among the factors to be considered.

        (i) N.B.: this case is the *majority rule*, which offers police a lower standard for their affidavits.

        (ii) N.B.: probable cause based on the "totality of the circumstances" requires the alleged occurrence not to have taken place too remotely in the past. Otherwise, there will be no probable cause to justify that the evidence will still be present.

        (iii) N.B.: although this case states the constitutional minimum, some states, wishing to grant the defendants greater protection, continue to use the *Aguilar-Spinelli test*, which remains the *minority rule* in 8 states.

2.4 Challenging the Warrant: the Four Corners Rule

2.4.1 In evaluating whether a warrant was supported by probable cause, the appeals court is limited to looking at *only the information* contained in the affidavit and warrant.

2.4.2 What was said to the magistrate is irrelevant if it was not in writing. *Franks v. Delaware* (U.S. 1978) (Blackmun, J.).

2.4.3 If the affidavit and warrant together do not give sufficient facts to form probable cause, the warrant is invalid.

2.4.4 Information given to the magistrate that is **deliberately false** or that **recklessly disregards the truth** voids the warrant.

2.4.5 The defendant has the burden of overcoming by a preponderance of the evidence a presumption that the warrant is valid.

2.5 Executing the Warrant

2.5.1 Time of Execution

    (a) The Constitution requires execution of the warrant within reasonable time under the circumstances.

    (b) Some states have statutes limiting this period even further, with some requiring execution in as little as ten days.

2.5.2 Notice

    (a) Traditionally, police officers were not required to knock on the door and announce their presence.

(b) However, after *Wilson v. Arkansas* (U.S. 1995), a "reasonableness standard" requiring police to knock, identify themselves, and give a copy of the search warrant was imposed.

    (i) However, the exclusionary rule does not apply to a knock and announce violation.

    (ii) See *Hudson v. Michigan* (U.S. 2006), where the court held that although *Wilson* is still good law, the knock and announce provision is not required by the constitution. Other remedies are available, such as suing the police for damages.

(c) Police may apply for a **no-knock warrant** if they state, for example, that there is a high risk of danger or that the evidence may be destroyed if they knock and announce their presence.

2.5.3 Scope of the Search

(a) A warrant to search the house includes the right to search all of the curtilage (the dwelling and all buildings and property immediately surrounding it).

(b) If, while searching for something inside of a house, there are other people present, it is reasonable to segregate them for just long enough to ascertain their involvement in the potential crime and to prevent any interference with the search.

(c) Upon conclusion of the search, they may be arrested or let go.

3 Exceptions to the Invalidity of Warrantless Searches and Seizures

3.1.1 Under *Illinois v. Gates* (U.S. 1983), a search warrant is generally required and searches realized without a warrant are presumed to be invalid. *Mincey v. Arizona* (U.S. 1978).

3.1.2 However, as we will examine in this section, there are several notable exceptions to these general rules.

3.2 Search Incident to Lawful Arrest

3.2.1 If the defendant is already being arrested, *no additional search warrant is necessary*.

3.2.2 Under *Weeks v. United States* (U.S. 1914) (Day, J.), the probable cause for the arrest is imported as probable for the search; separate probable cause is not necessary.

3.2.3 If the arrest is invalid, then so too is the search, since both are based on the same probable cause.

3.2.4 There are two reasons justifying a search:

(a) The *officer's protection*; and

(b) To *secure evidence* before it is destroyed.

3.2.5 Under these circumstances, the officer does not need to actually fear for his safety or have any reasonable suspicion that illegal materials will be found; once a lawful arrest is effected, a search is permitted.

3.2.6 Police may search the **arrestee's person** and the area within his **immediate control**.

(a) The rationale is to prevent the destruction of evidence within the defendant's **"wingspan."**

(b) *See Chimel v. California* (U.S. 1969) (Stewart, J.), where a warrantless search of the defendant's entire house after his arrest was held unconstitutional. The permitted scope of a search incident to lawful arrest is the area under the defendant's immediate control, known as the **"Chimel Perimeter."**

3.2.7 However, *when police have reasonable suspicion* and they arrest the defendant in his home for a violent crime, they may search his entire home. *Maryland v. Buie* (U.S. 1990).

3.2.8 If police arrest a criminal for one offense, and in the course of a search incident to lawful arrest, they find evidence of a separate, unrelated crime, that evidence is admissible. *United States v. Robinson* (U.S. 1973) (Rehnquist, J.) (heroin was recovered while an officer searched a man who was arrested for a traffic violation).

3.2.9 However, searches incident to lawful arrest apply *only when the defendant is arrested*. Police may not search the defendants during mere traffic stops.

(a) *See Knowles v. Iowa* (U.S. 1998) (Rehnquist), where the officer stopped the defendant, issued a summons, and sent him on his way. A search was not permitted because there was no full-blown arrest.

3.3 The Carroll Doctrine/Automobile Exception

3.3.1 A separate exception allowing for warrantless searches applies only to automobiles and other mobile vehicles (planes, boats, etc.).

3.3.2 Since these vehicles are mobile, requiring police to obtain a warrant before searching them gives rise to the risk that the evidence, along with the vehicles, will disappear.

3.3.3 This exception applies, even if there has been no arrest, when police have **probable cause** to believe a crime is being committed.

(a) *See Carroll v. United States* (U.S. 1925) (Taft, C.J.), where police were permitted to search the trunk of a car of a known bootlegger when they noticed the car heavily laden.

(b) N.B.: this case is the beginning of the **exigent circumstances doctrine**.

3.3.4 After an automobile is seized, police are not required to obtain a search warrant, since they could have searched it at the time it was stopped.

3.3.5 This doctrine is justified by the fact that (i) cars and other mobile vehicles are primarily means of transportation; (ii) they are driven in plain view; and (iii) they are subject to heavy regulation. *Chambers v. Maroney* (U.S. 1970) (White, J.).

3.3.6 However, this rationale does not apply to closed objects, such as footlockers or trunks found within the car, since they are *not within plain view* and since they are intended for the *storage of personal effects*.

(a) Furthermore, since police may seize the objects before applying for a search warrant, the exigent circumstances inherent in automobiles does not apply.

(b) *See United States v. Chadwick* (U.S. 1977) (Burger, C.J.), where the Court excluded evidence obtained from a footlocker seized from a vehicle that was opened without a search warrant.

3.3.7 Although *Chadwick* gives heightened protection to suitcases and personal luggage, this protection does not apply to *containers* or *canisters* found inside the car when there is probable cause to warrant a search.

3.3.8 When police have probable cause to stop a car, they **may search the entire car** until they find the object of the probable cause. *United States v. Ross* (U.S. 1982) (Stevens, J.) (permitting police to search a film canister found in a vehicle, although they did not have a warrant).

3.4 Hot Pursuit

3.4.1 When pursuing a dangerous suspect and *time is of the essence*, police may conduct warrantless searches.

    (a) *See* Warden v. Hayden (U.S. 1967) (Brennan, J.), where police were informed that the defendant Hayden had entered a house after a crime was committed. The police entered the house, searched it, and found clothing in the washing machine matching the description of the suspect. The defendant challenged the admission of the evidence, since it was obtained without a warrant. Held: because speed was essential, the warrantless search was justified. The Fourth Amendment is about reasonableness; it does not require police to obtain a warrant when doing so would allow the defendant to escape.

3.4.2 Hot pursuit justifies entry when:

    (a) There is **probable cause** (always necessary for searches and seizures);

    (b) Under **exigent circumstances** justifying the warrantless search;

    (c) The pursuit begins from a place where the police have **a lawful right to be;** and

    (d) The legal violation is **serious** enough to justify a warrantless search.

3.5 The Emergency Doctrine

3.5.1 In emergency situations, police are not required to obtain a warrant.

    (a) *See Michigan v. Tyler* (U.S. 1978) (Stewart, J.), where a fire chief and detective discovered flammable liquid in plastic bags while the fire department responded to a fire in a department store. They went back shortly thereafter, while the fire was still being fought, and collected more evidence. Three weeks later, investigators again went of the scene of the crime. Held: no search warrant was necessary during the first two investigations because there was an emergency and the fire department was lawfully on the premises. However, the third investigation was unlawful because it took place three weeks after the emergency.

3.5.2 The emergency doctrine does not permit police to collect evidence of the crime scene if they do not obtain a warrant.

    (a) In *Mincey v. Arizona* (U.S. 1978) (Stewart, J.), the Court struck down an Arizona statute that allowed police to conduct investigations at crime scenes without a warrant. Held: the statute is unconstitutional; there is **no crime-scene exception.** If police have probable cause, they must obtain a search warrant. If they do not have probable cause, they need consent.

3.6 Exigent Circumstances

3.6.1 The exigent circumstances exception arises when:

(a) Police have **probable cause** that a crime has been committed; and

(b) Absent immediate action, the evidence would be **lost**.

(i) Standard: whether a reasonable person would expect the police to stop and obtain a warrant.

3.6.2 Body Searches

(a) If a defendant ingests drugs, the evidence of a crime, police may not **pump his stomach**, not because of a Fourth Amendment prohibition, but rather, because Fourteenth Amendment Due Process would be offended. *Rochin v. California* (U.S. 1952) (Frankfurter, J.).

(b) **Blood tests**, on the contrary, are not prohibited by the Fourteenth Amendment, since they are so commonplace that they do not offend ordinary sensibilities. *Breithaupt v. Abram* (U.S. 1957) (Clark, J.).

(c) Any body search, including blood samples and DNA tests, must meet the following three prong test:

(i) There is a **"clear indication"** that the search will result in the evidence being sought;

(ii) **Exigent circumstances** prevent the obtention of a warrant (*e.g.*, drugs in the blood will disappear); and

(iii) The search is done in a reasonable manner. *Schmerber v. California* (U.S. 1966) (Brennan, J.).

3.6.3 Border Searches and Airport Security Searches

(a) The Fourth Amendment applies only to searches and seizures *within the United States*. At the borders, with a reasonable suspicion on its own, a suspect may be detained and searched. Since the government has an interest in regulating who comes into the country, a search warrant is not necessary. *United States v. Montoya de Hernandez* (U.S. 1985) (Rehnquist, J.).

(b) Justification of this doctrine: at the borders, people have less expectation of privacy, there are exigent circumstances, and there is implied consent.

(c) Landlocked cities that have international flights landing in them, as well as cities with international shipping ports, are considered "borders" for the application of this rule.

3.6.4 Summary of Exigent Circumstances Exception

(a) There must be reason to believe (generally, probable cause, but in the case of border searches, a reasonable suspicion is sufficient) that an immediate search is necessary to prevent evidence from disappearing;

(b) The search is otherwise reasonable. For bodily intrusions, this means:

(i) The procedure is effective in obtaining the required evidence;

(ii) It does not cause significant pain or trauma; and

(iii) The medical procedures followed are appropriate and necessary.

3.7 Plain View Exception

3.7.1 The plain view doctrine is an exception to the rule that a warrant is necessary to effect *only a seizure* (this exception does not apply to warranty searches).

3.7.2 Police may seize an object under the plain view doctrine when the following three elements are met:

(a) The object is in ***plain view***;

(b) The probable cause must be ***immediately apparent*** without the need for a further search.

(i) *See Arizona v. Hicks* (U.S. 1987) (Scalia, J.), where police, while investigating an apartment where gunshots went off, noticed a new radio that stood out from the squalor. Picking it up to obtain its serial number, they developed probable cause as to its being stolen. Held: the evidence of the stolen radio is inadmissible, since the probable cause was not immediately apparent, but rather, required that the radio first be manipulated. "No search no matter how cursory is allowed under the Fourth Amendment to determine whether probable cause exists."

(c) The police must be ***in a place where they have a lawful right to be*** (*e.g.*, they may not be trespassers);

(i) An object is always in plain view from some vantage point; the question is whether it is in plain view from a place where police may lawfully be.

(1) In *Coolidge v. New Hampshire* (U.S. 1971) (Stewart, J.) (the source of the "neutral and detached magistrate" rule), police were unable to rely on a warrant because it was issued by the state's attorney general (chief prosecutor). Thus, in order to admit incriminating evidence found in the vehicle, the police needed an exception to the warrant requirement. Because the car was parked, the *Carroll* doctrine did not apply. The State therefore argued the plain view doctrine: the car was in plain view from the public street. The Court rejected this argument, since the police were not in a place where they had lawful right to be.

(ii) Mere Pretext Doctrine

(1) Evidence in plain view is admissible even if a stop for one legal violation was a *mere pretext* to stop and search the defendant for other violations.

(2) *See Whren v. United States* (U.S. 1996) (Scalia, J.), where police, based on traffic law violations, stopped a defendant drug dealer and observed contraband in plain view. The defendants claimed that the stop was only a pretext to search if the defendant had drugs on him, but the Court admitted the evidence.

(3) Exceptions to the pretext doctrine:

(aa) When the pretext is based on race or other protected classes;

(bb) When there is no probable cause to stop the vehicle or no other basis; and

(cc) Where the individual may be harmed (this would not occur in a traffic violation).

3.8 Frisk after Terry Stop

3.8.1 A person is arrested if his movement is restricted when he: (i) is *touched*; (ii) is taken into the *physical custody* of the officer; or (iii) *submits to the authority* of the officer. *California v. Hodari D.* (U.S. 1991).

3.8.2 A stop is a **brief detention for questioning;** it is somewhere between an encounter and an arrest. *Terry v. Ohio* (U.S. 1968).

3.8.3 To effect a stop, police do not need reasonable cause; all they require is a **"reasonable suspicion"** that "criminal activity is afoot."

(a) *See Terry v. Ohio* (U.S. 1968) (Warren, C.J.), where a police officer noticed three men acting suspiciously outside of a jewelry store at 3 a.m. He encountered them and asked them questions, but they did not respond. He patted them down and found two weapons. A conviction followed and the defendant attacked the stop and frisk on the grounds that there had been an arrest (restriction of movement), but *no probable cause* (no crime was committed). Held: a stop is to be distinguished from a full-blown arrest; probable cause is required for arrests, but is no longer required for stops, which are valid if there is a *reasonable suspicion* that criminal activity has happened, is happening, or will happen. The officer must *detain the suspect briefly for the purpose of investigation.*

3.8.4 If, after the stop, the police officer has a **reasonable suspicion** that the suspect is in **possession of a weapon**, the officer **may conduct a frisk** of the suspect. This is limited to **patting down the outer clothing** to find a concealed weapon in order to provide for the protection of the police officer.

3.8.5 Under the **plain feel doctrine,** if, during the frisk, the officer feels something that he believes to be contraband, this may become independent probable cause for conducting a search.

3.8.6 The post-*Terry* categories of police-citizen contacts can be summarized as follow:

(a) Arrest and search incident to a lawful arrest (requiring probable cause);

(b) Stop and frisk limited to a search for weapons (requiring a reasonable suspicion); and

(c) Encounters, in which the defendant feels that he has the liberty to leave (determined by the totality of the circumstances). *United States v. Mendenhall* (U.S. 1980) (Stewart, J.).

3.8.7 Automobile Stop and Frisk

(a) Reasonable suspicion also permits a stop and frisk of the driver of a car. *Pennsylvania v. Mimms* (U.S. 1977). It is reasonable to demand that he exit and be subject to a frisk.

(b) If there is reasonable suspicion that other **passengers** are armed, they too may be frisked. *Maryland v. Wilson* (U.S. 1997).

3.9 Consent

3.9.1 One's Fourth Amendment privacy right may be fully or partially waived, regardless of whether the party waiving the right knows that he has a right to refuse to do so. *Schneckloth v. Bustamonte* (U.S. 1973) (Stewart, J.).

3.9.2 The consent may be revoked at any time.

3.9.3 If unrestricted consent is given to a police officer to search a house or a car, then the police officer has the right to search the entire house.

   (a) However, even when an owner consents to a search without limitations, police are only permitted to search places where they could **reasonably find** the object sought. *Florida v. Jimeno* (U.S. 1991) (Rehnquist, C.J.).

   (b) This means that **police may only search where the object is likely to be found** (*e.g.*, they may not pry open a jewelry box to find a sterio). Police may also manipulate objects.

   (c) The scope of the search is limited to where a reasonable person would expect police to search.

3.9.4 The consent must be **voluntary**.

   (a) Courts are to look to the *totality of the circumstances* in determining whether consent was voluntary.

   (b) The fact that the defendants who consented to a search were minorities does not on its own indicate that consent was coerced. *United States v. Mendenhall United States v. Mendenhall* (U.S. 1980) (Stewart, J.) (rejecting an exception based on race).

3.9.5 Third Party Consent

   (a) If police enter a jointly occupied dwelling, either resident may consent to the police's search of any part of the dwelling where the other resident has no *Katz* reasonable expectation of privacy (*e.g.*, the common areas, a shared bedroom, etc.).

      (i) The key to this consent is **apparent authority**: police may rely on the consent of a third party who has apparent authority to consent to the search.

      (ii) If police act reasonably in their belief that the party had authority to consent, the exclusionary rule will not apply, even if the police's judgment was erroneous.

   (b) However, if either resident occupies his own separate bedroom or living space, his privacy to that space may not be waived by another resident, since he has a continued *Katz* reasonable expectation of privacy.

   (c) Furthermore, if one resident consents to a search of the house, but another resident who is also physically present and who has an equal expectation of privacy objects to the search, police are not permitted to conduct the search. *Randolph v. Georgia* (U.S. 2006) (Souter, J.).

3.10 Regulatory Searches

3.10.1 Traditionally, it was thought that the Fourth Amendment applied only to criminal searches and seizures.

3.10.2 However, *Camara v. Municipal Court* (U.S. 1967) (White, J.) established that regulatory inspections, such as inspections for housing code violations, were also within the scope of the Fourth Amendment

3.10.3 Thus, regulatory searches also require warrants, but unlike criminal search warrants, regulatory search warrants do not require **probable cause**, since it is impractical to expect the government to support an affidavit with probable cause, which usually only arises *after the warrant is issued* and the government is permitted to inspect the premises.

    (a)   *N.B.*: if there are exigent circumstances, no regulatory warrant is necessary.

3.10.4 Thus, although the regulatory purpose exception requires a warrant, it does not require probable cause to obtain the warrant.

3.11 Special Needs Situations

3.11.1 In the following situations, special needs justify not having to obtain a warrant.

3.11.2 Public Schools

    (a)   Because of the *special need* of keeping students safe in public schools, officials require neither a warrant nor probable cause to effect a search or seizure.

    (b)   *See New Jersey v. T.L.O.* (U.S. 1985) (White, J.), where the Court upheld the rights of public school officials to search students with neither warrants nor probable cause. Mere suspicion was sufficient. The Court drew a distinction between police officers and school officials, and held that the latter are not held to the same standards as the former, given the **need to maintain the safety of the school environment**. Furthermore, when an educator suspects a student of possessing contraband, time is of the essence and it is not practical to expect the school official to obtain a warrant.

3.11.3 Parolees and Probationers

    (a)   Police may conduct unannounced searches and seizures of parolees (Executive Branch) and probationers (Judicial Branch) as a condition of their release.

    (b)   Parolees and probationers have a lessened expectation of privacy, since their freedom is conditional.

3.11.4 Drug Testing of Government Employees and Officials

    (a)   These drug tests may be conducted absent a warrant because of the special need of assuring society that its law enforcement and public officials are drug-free.

3.12 Community Caretaker/Inventory Search

3.12.1 This exception is different from other exceptions to the requirement for a warrant in that it is based not on a law enforcement purpose, but rather, on community care: the purpose is to protect the community.

(a) *See Cady v. Dombrowski* (U.S. 1973) (Rehnquist, C.J.), where police officers arrested the defendant, a corrupt Chicago cop, and towed his car to a private garage. When they later realized that his gun was likely in the car, they went to remove it and in the process, discovered incriminating evidence. Held: the evidence is admissible even though police did not have probable cause to search the car: care of the community permits officers to assure that guns are not left in unattended vehicles.

3.12.2 Once legally in their possession, police may inventory all effects without a search warrant.

(a) In *South Dakota v. Opperman* (U.S. 1976) (Burger, C.J.), the court extended the right to search impounded vehicles, regardless of whether dangerous objects were suspected to be in the car, in order to: (i) protect the belongings of the defendant from theft; and (ii) to protect police from liability accusations that the defendant's property was stolen.

3.13 Search and Seizure Analysis Sumary

3.13.1 When analyzing search and seizure questions, first ask if there was a search or seizure.

3.13.2 If there was, apply the following analysis:

(a) Does the Fourth Amendment apply (was the search/seizure unreasonable?)?

(b) Was a warrant necessary?

(c) If so, was there a search or seizure/arrest warrant?

(d) Was there probable cause?

(e) Was the warrant valid?

(f) Was the scope of the warrant exceeded?

(g) Did an exception to the warrant/probable cause requirements apply? (Search incident to lawful arrest; Carroll Doctrine/automobile exception; plain view; Frisk after *Terry* stop; consent; regulatory purpose).

(h) If not complied with, what is the remedy?

4 The Fifth Amendment Double Jeopardy Clause

4.1 Introduction

4.1.1 The Fifth Amendment requires that no person "be subject for the same offence to be twice put in jeopardy of life or limb."

4.1.2 Major issues surrounding the Double Jeopardy Clause include the following:

(a) Does it apply to only some or all criminal offenses?

(b) Does it apply only in the trial or also in the appeal?

(c) What if there is a guilty plea and there is no trial?

4.1.3 Under the common law, if a defendant has been acquitted or convicted of a crime, he cannot be retried. These principles are referred to as ***autre fois conviction*** and ***autre fois acquittal***, respectively.

4.1.4 Since *autre fois conviction* and *autre fois acquittal* were already prohibited under the common law, Madison believed that the Double Jeopardy Clause was unnecessary.

4.1.5 Today, however, the Double Jeopardy Clause also prevents the defendant from being *punished for the same offense* more than once.

4.1.6 The Double Jeopardy Clause applies to both the federal government and to the states through the Fourteenth Amendment Due Process Clause. *Benton v. Maryland* (U.S. 1969) (Marshall, J.).

4.2 When Jeopardy Attaches

4.2.1 Jeopardy attaches when the trial begins—which is when the ***jury is impaneled, takes the oath, and is sworn in***. *Crist v. Betz* (U.S. 1978) (Stewart, J.).

4.2.2 However, at a bench trial with no jury, jeopardy attaches when the first witness is ***sworn in*** and ***testifies***.

4.2.3 Anytime before then, jeopardy does not attach. The prosecutor may stop and start over again without implicating the Double Jeopardy Clause.

4.2.4 When there is no trial and the defendant pleads guilty, jeopardy attaches when the judge determines that the plea is entered knowingly and willingly and the judgment becomes final.

4.3 When Jeopardy Applies

4.3.1 Double jeopardy applies only to criminal cases whose sanctions threatan "life or limb."

4.3.2 The Legislative Branch defines when a case is criminal.

  (a) *See Hudson v. United States* (U.S. 1997) (Rehnquist, C.J.), where the defendant had been charged and acquitted of a crime. The government then filed a forfeiture action for the defendant's ill-gotten gains. The defendant argued that he was being twice punished. Held: the legislature did indicate that this forfeiture case was criminal and the ***courts should not second guess legislature***, since there are no indicia showing the case to be criminal (*e.g.*, a "guilty beyond a reasonable doubt" evidentiary standard). The action is civil and the Double Jeopardy Clause does not apply.

4.4 Special Contexts

4.4.1 When the Double Jeopardy Clause Does Not Apply

  (a) Under the doctrine of ***manifest necessity***, the Double Jeopardy Clause does not prohibit a retrial.

  (b) Manifest necessity applies in two situations:

    (i) A Mistrial is Caused by the Defendant's Conduct

      (1) When a mistrial is caused by the misconduct of the defendant or that of his attorney, double jeopardy does not apply.

4. THE FIFTH AMENDMENT DOUBLE JEOPARDY CLAUSE

          (2)   The rationale of this rule is that the defendant should not be able to benefit from his causing a mistrial.

    (ii)   Hung Juries

          (1)   When the jury is unable to arrive at a unanimous verdict that is legally mandated in most states,[1] double jeopardy does not apply.

          (2)   The defendant may be retried, since neither a conviction nor an acquittal has been entered.

          (3)   The retrial is simply viewed as a continuation of the first trial.

(c)   The founders intended the Double Jeopardy Clause to protect defendants when there has been a full and fair trial. Where there is a hung jury or a mistrial caused by the defendant's misconduct, there has been no full and fair trial. *Illinois v. Somerville* (U.S. 1973) (Rehnquist, J.).

4.4.2 When the Double Jeopardy Clause Does Apply

(a)   The Double Jeopardy Clause does apply when a mistrial is caused by the prosecutor's misconduct.

(b)   In this situation, the court must look at the nature of the misconduct.

(c)   Merely negligent conduct causing a mistrial and a retrial does not offend double jeopardy.

(d)   However, if the prosecution deliberately causes a mistrial or intentionally goads the defense into moving for a mistrial, double jeopardy would be implicated in a retrial. *Oregon v. Kennedy* (U.S. 1982) (Rehnquist, J.).

(e)   If the prosecutor's own personal behavior is not the direct cause of a mistrial, it is not clear if double jeopardy will apply in a retrial.

    (i)   Example: a prosecutor's witness blurts out "the defendant confessed" with respect to an inadmissible confession. The court declares a mistrial.

    (ii)   Several factors will be considered as to whether a retrial can be heard (*e.g.*, whether whether the prosecutor put the witness up to making the statement).

4.5 Collateral Estoppel and Double Jeopardy

4.5.1 Introduction

(a)   Collateral estoppel[2] (issue preclusion) prohibits an issue that has been judicially resolved between two parties from being relitigated.

(b)   The earlier judgment is to be binding on the parties implicated in the original adjudication.

---

[1] Colloquially referred to as a "hung jury."
[2] This idea is closely related to claim preclusion (*res judicata*, "the thing is adjudicated"), which deals not with relitigating the same issue, but rather, the same claim that was litigated or could have been litigated in a prior suit that reached a final judgment.

4.5.2 Lesser Included Offenses

(a) Two offenses are considered the same offense for the purpose of jeopardy, *unless each of them contains an element not included in the other.*

(b) If they include the same elements or if one offense contains all of the elements of a lesser included offense, then double jeopardy bars relitigation of one after the other has reached a verdict (this includes trials for a lesser included offense if the defendant was already acquitted for the greater offense, *see infra.*).

(c) If, however, each offense has some unique element, then it is not the same offense for double jeopardy purposes. Since they are not the same offense, the defendant can be prosecuted separately for each offense without violating the Double Jeopardy Clause. *Blockburger v. United States* (U.S. 1932) (Sutherland, J.).

4.5.3 Examples Where Jeopardy Attaches

(a) The defendant is acquitted of second degree murder and is then tried for first degree murder.

　(i) Since these offenses do not each contain some unique element (second degree murder is a lesser included offense within first degree murder), they are not separate offenses.

　(ii) Therefore, once jeopardy attaches for second degree murder, the defendant cannot be prosecuted for first degree murder (this rule applies regardless of which offense is tried first).

　(iii) This is because, once the defendant has been acquitted in the trial for second degree murder, it is implied that he is also acquitted for all lesser included crimes.

　(iv) Bringing a later case for a lesser included crime would violate double jeopardy.

(b) The defendant is charged with first degree murder and is convicted of second degree murder. He cannot be again charged with first degree murder.

　(i) Although no verdict was entered with respect to the first degree murder, a conviction on the lesser included charge of second degree murder implies an acquittal on the greater offense.

　(ii) Trying him again would be like trying him for an offense after a "verdict" of "not guilty" has already been entered. *Price v. Georgia* (U.S. 1970).

(c) The defendant is acquitted of felony murder and is later charged with the underlying felony.

　(i) Except for in rare circumstances, the defendant cannot be tried separately for felony murder as well as for the underlying felony.

　(ii) Since proving the felony does not require the plaintiff to prove any additional facts not already proved when the plaintiff shows the felony murder itself, the felony is a lesser included offense.

　(iii) Therefore, reprosecuting the defendant for that offense would constitute double jeopardy.

4.5.4 Examples of Separate Offenses Where Jeopardy Does Not Attach

(a) DUI and involuntary manslaughter;

(b) Multiple robberies (each of which can be tried separately).

4.5.5 Modern Test

(a) *Brady v. Corbin* (U.S. 1990) overruled *Blockburger*, but *Brady* was then reversed by *United States v. Dixon* (U.S. 1993), which reinstituted the *Blockburger* test: **unless each offense has one or more distinct elements, they are the same offense**.

(b) Today, the "same elements test" under *Blockburger* must be applied and it must be determined whether the legislature *clearly intended multiple punishments* for the same offense. If so, there is no double jeopardy problem.

   (i) In *Missouri v. Hunter* (U.S. 1983) (Burger, C.J.), the defendant was convicted under one statute and then prosecuted and convicted under a second statute having the same elements. Held: under *Blockburger*, the two crimes are the same offense. However, it was clear from the record that the Missouri legislature intended for defendants to be prosecuted for both of them. Judgment for the defendant reversed.

4.6 Dual Sovereignty Doctrine

4.6.1
When a defendant's conduct violates both federal and state law, a double jeopardy problem will not arise if he is prosecuted by both the federal and state government.

4.6.2
Rationale: the federal government and every state is a separate sovereign, and the Double Jeopardy Clause is intended to prevent multiple prosecutions of a defendant for the same offense **by the same sovereign.**

4.6.3
Where there is the **same conduct**, a crime is not considered the "**same offense**" when punished by the state and federal governments separately.

(a) In *Bartkus v. Illinois* (U.S. 1959) (Frankfurter, J.), the defendant was charged with robbery and was acquitted in federal court. Later, the local state prosecutor indicted and convicted the defendant with the same facts and witnesses as those used in federal court. Held: every citizen may be liable to punishment for an infraction of the laws of both his state and federal government. By one act, he may be tried and punished for two offenses.

(b) *N.B.*: although the Constitution would not be offended by these double prosecutions, some states have imposed limitations on *state prosecutions brought after federal prosecutions*.

4.6.4
Double jeopardy does not prevent different states from trying the same offense.

(a) In *Heath v. Alabama* (U.S. 1985) (O'Connor, J.), the defendant hired two men to kill his wife. He was later charged in Georgia, where he received a life sentence, and later in Alabama by a prosecutor who believed he deserved the death penalty. Held: double jeopardy is not offended when a defendant is prosecuted by two states when he has violated the laws of both of them.

4.7   Appeals

4.7.1   Appeals, which are permitted in every state, are not constitutionally mandated. Nowhere in the Bill of Rights is the word "appeal" used. However, if the state is to give an appeal, it must honor due process.

4.7.2   Appeals by the Defendant

    (a)   When the defendant appeals his conviction and it is overturned, one of two things is possible:

        (i)   There was *insufficient evidence* as a matter of law, in which case double jeopardy attaches and retrial is prohibited. The trial court should have entered a verdict of acquittal; or

        (ii)   The *trial court erred*, in which case a retrial is permitted, since the defendant, in appealing, waives his double jeopardy right and the jeopardy is simply continuing from the original trial. *Burks v. United States* (U.S. 1978) (Burger, C.J.).

            (1)   In *Green v. United States* (U.S. 1957) (Black, J.), the defendant appealed his conviction and the appeals court found that the trial court erred and remanded the case. The defendant appealed, arguing that the Double Jeopardy Clause was violated. Held: an appeal by a defendant either (i) constitutes a *waiver of the double jeopardy right* (the defendant is implying that he wants a new trial because the trial court erred); or (ii) is a *continuation of the trial* if it is sent back to trial on remand.

4.7.3   Appeals by the Prosecution

    (a)   Prosecutorial appeals are not constitutionally prohibited, but they are constrained by the Double Jeopardy Clause and Speedy Trial Clause.

    (b)   When the prosecution appeals pre-trial, there is no jeopardy issue.

    (c)   In states that allow post-trial appeals by the state, the Double Jeopardy Clause applies.

        (i)   A waiver theory would not apply, since it is not the defendant who is appealing.

        (ii)   There are two kinds of appeals:

            (1)   Stand-in Appeals

                (aa)   The prosecution notes an appeal, but the defendant can not be tried again.

                (bb)   The appeal goes up in his name but he has no risk, since the state is asking for an advisory opinion for future cases.

                (cc)   There is no effect on the defendant's acquittal or conviction.

            (2)   *Interlocutory Appeal*

                (aa)   Interlocutory appeals apply only while the case is pending.

(d) Standard of Review for Constitutional Error

   (i) An error is harmless only if it had minimal effect or did not not affect the jury. *Kotteakos v. United States* (U.S. 1946).

   (ii) Proving harmless error is a high bar to overcome **requiring *proof beyond a reasonable doubt*.**

   (1) *See Chapman v. California* (U.S. 1967) (Black, J.), where the prosecution was required to show on appeal, beyond a reasonable doubt, that the error did not contribute to the verdict.

   (iii) Error is never harmless when the following rights are violated:

   (1) The Fifth Amendment right against double jeopardy; and

   (2) The Sixth Amendment rights to a speedy trial by an impartial jury, and to the assistance of counsel.

4.8 Retroactivity

4.8.1 Traditionally, any new constitutional holding was to apply to any case active in the system (all cases on appeal or in habeas) at the time of the ruling.

4.8.2 This rule changed with *Linkletter v. Walker* (U.S. 1965) (Clark, J.), where the Court recognized that the traditional rule caused exorbitant costs and time expenditures on the parties. Under the new approach, a new rule is to be applied retroactively when the Court makes this clear when stating the rule; otherwise, the courts are to apply the rule retroactively when it is practical.

5 The Fifth Amendment Self-Incrimination Clause

5.1 Overview of The Privilege

5.1.1 The Fifth Amendment Self-Incrimination Clause guarantees that no person shall be compelled by the ***government*** in any criminal case to be a witness (must be ***testimonial*** in nature) against himself (it is strictly ***personal***).

5.1.2 There Must Be Testimony

   (a) The privilege applies to evidence that is testimonial in nature, including the defendant's statements, documents and records, but does not apply to evidence that is ***real and demonstrable*** (*e.g.* hair, blood, fingerprints, photographs, signatures).

   (b) The test: testimony must be ***an assertion of fact that is either true or false***, *Schmerber v. California* (U.S. 1966) (Brennan, J.), but one's ***name and identification*** is not considered to be testimonial, since there is nothing incriminating about it. *Hiibel v. Sixth Judicial District Court of Nevada* (U.S. 2004).

   (c) Furthermore, the prosecution may generally obtain preexisting business records (*e.g.*, income tax statements, bank statements, etc.) that were voluntarily prepared by the defendant.

5.1.3 When the Privilege Applies

(a) Future Risk of Incrimination

(i) The privilege applies not only to criminal cases, but to any proceeding in which a future criminal prosecution may occur.

(1) *See Lefkowitz v. Turley* (U.S. 1973) (White, J.), where the Court held that requiring a defendant to testify when criminal charges could be made would be to subject him to a "cruel trilemna" of choosing between compelled testimony, perjury, or contempt of court.

(ii) In civil cases, when a witness faces no potential criminal charges (*e.g.*, he has already been tried and acquitted), he may be forced to testify. *Piemonte v. United States* (U.S. 1961).

(iii) It is not for the courts to determine whether charges are criminal or civil; rather, it is for the legislature.

(1) *See United States v. Ward* (U.S. 1980) (Rehnquist, J.), where the Court held that a penalty for polluting was not criminal because Congress had so expressed.

(iv) Several factors can be used to ascertain whether the legislature intended for a statute to be criminal or civil, including the penalties (prison versus a fine); and the burden of proof (beyond a reasonable doubt versus preponderance).

(b) State Action

(i) The constitutional protections apply only to government violations, not to violations by private actors.

(ii) Thus, if a defendant confesses to a friend who then gives the information to the police, there is no Fifth Amendment violation.

(iii) If, however, a "false friend" is planted by the police, that person becomes a police agent and the Fifth Amendment applies.

(c) Only Natural Persons Are Protected

(i) The privilege against self-incrimination applies only to natural, not legal persons.

(ii) *See Braswell v. United States* (U.S. 1988), holding that the Fifth Amendment is inapplicable to a closely-held corporation.

(d) Government Informants

(i) The privilege does not apply when a defendant assumes the risk of confiding to a "friend," who may be a government informant. *Hoffa v. United States* (U.S. 1966).

(e) Before a Subpoena Is Served

(i) When documents are prepared before a government subpoena is served, they are not protected under the Fifth Amendment. *See Fisher v. United States* (U.S. 1976) (White, J.) (overruling *Boyd v. United States*).

5.2 The *Miranda* Safeguards

5.2.1 The case *Miranda v. Arizona* (U.S. 1966) guarantees that defendants in police custody will be informed of the following four rights and warnings:

(a) The right to remain silent;

(b) The right to consult with an attorney and to have the attorney present during questioning;

(c) The right to court-appointed counsel if he is indigent; and

(d) That anything that defendants say can or will be used against them in court.

5.2.2 The Functions of the Warnings

(a) To enable suspects to make an "intelligent decision" regarding the exercise of constitutional rights.

(b) To make suspects "acutely aware" that they are "not in the presence of people acting in their sole interest."

5.2.3 Constructive Violations

(a) In closing arguments, prosecutors ***may not comment on the defendant's failure to testify.*** Doing so constructively violates the Fifth Amendment by compelling him to testify. Prosecutors may, however, state that evidence was uncontradicted. *Griffin v. California* (U.S. 1965).

(b) If, however, the defendant ***invites*** such comments, the privilege is waived.

(i) *See United States v. Robinson* (U.S. 1988) (Rehnquist, C.J.), where the defendant's attorney said that the government did not give the defendant the opportunity to present his side of the story. The prosecutor was permitted to respond that the defendant failed to avail himself of the opportunity to testify.

5.2.4 Deception and Misrepresentation

(a) The Fifth Amendment ***does not prohibit police from deceiving suspects*** by planting "false friends" in order to elicit confessions.

(i) *See Frazier v. Cupp* (U.S. 1969) (Marshall, J.), where the Court permitted police to lie in telling the defendant that a second defendant confessed. *There is nothing coercive about hearing that a friend confessed.*

(b) However, police may not trick the defendants into confessing by falsely offering to drop charges.

5.3 The Two-Prong Threshold Test

5.3.1 Determining *whether statements are admissible* under the Fifth Amendment Privilege against Self-Incrimination requires a threshold test.

5.3.2 First, *determine if the confession was voluntary.*

    (a) There are three factors to consider when determining whether a confession is involuntary.

        (i) **Police Conduct**. A confession is involuntary when it is the result of police torture, threats of violence, repeatedly denying requests for a lawyer, psychological coercion, or other acts that "overbear the will" of the suspect (*i.e.*, cause him to confess not because the confession is true, but because it is what the law enforcement officials wished to hear).

        (ii) **Characteristics of the suspect**, such as his age, injuries, mental capacities, and mental state.

        (iii) **Surrounding circumstances**, including the length of an interrogation; the lack of food or rest; and the degree of isolation from family, friends, and counsel.

    (b) If it is determined that a confession is involuntary, it is inadmissible under the Due Process Clause.

        (i) *See Brown v. Mississippi* (U.S. 1936), where the defendants confessed only after brutal beatings by the police. The Court held that the confessions were not voluntary and were therefore inadmissible.

5.3.3 If it is determined that the confession was voluntary, move onto the *Miranda* prong: any statements given to the police will be excluded if the *Miranda* warnings were not first read when the statements are both:

    (a) Made while the suspect was in **police custody**;

    (b) During a police **interrogation**.

5.4 Custody and Interrogation

5.4.1 The Requirement of Custody

    (a) The *Miranda* warnings apply only when the defendant is in police custody.

    (b) A person is in custody when he *reasonably believes* that he is *not free to leave. Orozco v. Texas* (U.S. 1969).

    (c) Although the test is objective, it considers what is reasonable from the perspective of a reasonable person in the defendant's circumstances.

        (i) *See Berkemer v. McCarty* (U.S. 1984) (Marshall, J.), where the court held that *even if an officer planned on arresting a defendant* in a routine traffic stop, the defendant was not in custody if a reasonable person in his position would not have understood the traffic stop to have meant that he would be arrested. *It is measured from the reasonable suspect's perception* of the situation, not from the officer's reasoning and thinking.

(d) For the purposes of *Miranda*, questioning on the scene regarding the facts of a crime during fact-finding does not meet the requirement of custody.

5.4.2 The Requirement of an Interrogation

(a) Once it is shown that the defendant was in custody, the defense must also argue that an actual interrogation took place.

(b) A confession that is completely voluntary, without even a single interrogation by police, need not be excluded.

(i) See *Colorado v. Connelly* (U.S. 1986) (Rehnquist, C.J.), where the Court did not exclude evidence of a defendant who made incriminating statements while in a room with a video monitor even though police did not read him his *Miranda* rights, since there was no police interrogation. The police simply put the defendant in the room and video monitored him for his own safety, since he showed the symptoms of a mental disorder.

(c) The interrogation relates to testimonial information, not real and demonstrable evidence, such as name, social security number, and other identification information.

(d) It applies not only to the questioning of the defendant, but also to any words or actions by police other than those involved in **booking**. *Illinois v. Perkins* (U.S. 1990) (Kennedy, J.) (affirming and amplifying *Rhode Island v. Innis* (U.S. 1980)).

(e) An interrogation may thus be comprised of police conduct without actual questioning as well as police statements seeking to ascertain information.

(i) For example, not only direct questions, but also statements such as "tell me more" are considered to be interrogation.

(ii) Furthermore, the statement by a police officer in the presence of the defendant that all he wanted to do was enable the family of a missing victim a "Christian burial" for their ten year old girl, because it was designed to elicit incriminating statements by the defendant, was held to be an interrogation requiring the *Miranda* warnings in *Nix v. Williams* (U.S. 1984).

(f) Volunteered Statements

(i) If the defendant offers incriminating testimony before there is ever an interrogation, the evidence will not be excluded on the basis of the *Miranda* rights having not been read.

(1) See *Pennsylvania v. Muniz* (U.S. 1990) (Brennan, J.), where the Court admitted confessions made by a drunk defendant, since there was never an actual police interrogation. The officer only asked for identifying information and then asked the defendant if he understood the officer's explanations as to taking a breathalyzer test.

(aa) *N.B.*: the dissent focused on the defendant's having been drunk as a strong factor against admissibility.

(2) *See also United States v. Patane* (U.S. 2004) (Thomas, J.), where the defendant interrupted police while they were advising him of his rights and and told them that he knew what his rights were. The Court did not exclude evidence of a gun because the defendant volunteered its whereabouts to the police.

(ii) Furthermore, statements that are not responsive to a question asked, are not to be excluded under *Miranda*. *Rhode Island v. Innis* (U.S. 1980).

5.5 The Exclusionary Remedy

5.5.1 The Prophylactic Remedy

(a) Before *Miranda v. Arizona* was decided in 1966, the **McNabb-Mallory Rule** required that evidence violating the Fifth Amendment be excluded in federal court. *McNabb v. United States* (U.S. 1943); *Mallory v. United States* (U.S. 1957).

(b) Since the *McNabb-Mallory* Rule was not a constitutional doctrine, Congress had the power to overrule it, which it did in 18 USC § 3501.

(c) The Supreme Court later held that 18 USC § 3501 was unconstitutional because it failed to require police to adequately inform the defendants of their rights (*e.g.*, the right to counsel).

(d) *Miranda v. Arizona* (U.S. 1966) established a new test looking to the totality of the circumstances in determining whether a confession was voluntary. If a confession *is not voluntary,* or is voluntary but the defendant was not read the *Miranda* warnings during an interrogation in police custody, **the confession must be excluded**.

(e) The rule is not constitutional; it is a **prophylactic rule** that carries the same remedies as constitutional rules.

(i) *See Miranda v. Arizona* (U.S. 1966) (Warren, C.J.), where the Court reversed the conviction of the defendant, who had been *interrogated* without being advised of his right to remain silent or have an attorney present. The Court held that once a defendant requests an attorney, the interrogation must cease until an attorney is present. Although this is *not a constitutional rule*, it is treated as one in order to *protect the constitutional right against self-incrimination*. It is to be applied until Congress and the states come up with a better rule.

(ii) Dissent (Harlan, J.): the required warnings will decrease confessions. There is no constitutional precedent for what the majority is doing and it is unwise as a matter of public policy.

(iii) *N.B.:* the dissents (JJ. Clark, Harlan, White, Stewart) disagreed as to what could be done as an alternative. Clark combined what they agreed upon and wrote it into a dissent. The chief disagreement was the *new right to counsel in the Fifth Amendment* that was created by the majority.

(iv) *N.B.:* after this decision, the states were incensed and many tried to impeach Chief Justice Warren. Congress tried to reverse the holding via statute, but the DOJ has rarely enforced it.

5.5.2 The Constitutional Rule

(a) Although originally, Chief Justice Warren made it clear that *Miranda* was not to be a constitutional rule, this later changed.

(b) In 2000, the Court held in *United States v. Dickerson* (U.S. 2000) (Rehnquist, C.J.) that because the states and Congress had not accepted the Court's prior invitation to come up with a better rule than that pronounced in *Miranda v. Arizona* (U.S. 1966), the **Miranda Rule is now a constitutional rule.**

5.5.3 Reversible Error

(a) If a court errs by allowing an inadmissible confession into evidence, a conviction will be reversed and a new trial will be ordered **if the error was material** (*i.e.*, outcome determinative). *Arizona v. Fulminante* (U.S. 1991).

(b) If, however, the admission of an inadmissible confession was **harmless error** (*e.g.*, there was so much evidence that the defendant was inevitably going to be convicted), the conviction will stand.

5.5.4 Limited Uses of Excluded Confessions

(a) Although involuntary confessions are generally inadmissible, *they may be used to impeach* the defendant's testimony. *Harris v. New York* (U.S. 1971).

(b) Furthermore, confessions given *after the defendant has invoked his right to counsel*, even thought they are generally inadmissible, may be used to impeach the defendant's testimony. *Oregon v. Hass* (U.S. 1975).

5.6 Public Safety Exception to Exclusion

5.6.1 A court is not required to exclude evidence obtained without the *Miranda* warnings when **"overriding considerations of public safety"** warrant an interrogation without the *Miranda* safeguards.

5.6.2 A court is to weigh the following factors in a balancing test:

(a) *Public safety considerations* from the perspective of a reasonable police officer; against

(b) The *need for a prophylactic rule* designed to protect the Fifth Amendment right again self-incrimination.

5.6.3 *See New York v. Quarles* (U.S. 1984) (Rehnquist, J.), where police seize the defendant after he robbed a store. When they saw that he was wearing a gun belt but had no gun, they asked him where the abandoned gun was before they read him the *Miranda* warnings. Held: the *Miranda* warnings are not necessary under public safety emergencies. Here, there was a presumably loaded gun in a grocery store with small children who could access it. The public safety considerations outweigh the need for the warnings.

5.7 Purging an Illegal Confession Through a Repeat Confession

5.7.1   If police interrogate the defendant while he is in custody without reading him the *Miranda* warnings and obtain a confession, they may read the defendant his *Miranda* rights and interrogate him afresh in order to "purge" the confession from its taint.

5.7.2   If the defendant again confesses, the confession is admissible if it is **knowing and voluntary.**

   (a)   See *Oregon v. Elstad* (U.S. 1985) (O'Connor), where the defendant made incriminating statements before police read him his *Miranda* warnings. When police later read him his *Miranda* rights, he waived them and again confessed. Held: *the voluntary and knowing waiver* cured any taint from the earlier confession.

5.8 The "Fruit of the Poisonous Tree" within the *Miranda* Context

5.8.1   The illegal fruit of confessions that violate *Miranda* is not required to be suppressed; the fruit of the poisonous tree doctrine does not apply to evidence obtained because of violations of *Miranda*.

   (a)   Originally, this holding was based on the theory that the *Miranda* warnings were merely prophylactic safeguards, not constitutional rights; therefore, the Court had the discretion to fashion the remedy as it wished.

   (b)   However, after *Dickerson* constitutionalized *Miranda*, the rationale for the admissibility of fruits of a *Miranda* violation is that the court has created an **exception** to the rule.

   (c)   Many police took advantage of this by illegally seeking confessions that would be suppressed in order to obtain new evidence that would not be suppressed as fruit of the poisonous tree.

5.8.2   Only Good Faith Error Permitted

   (a)   This eventually led to *Missouri v. Seibert* (U.S. 2004), which held that the fruit of a *Miranda* violation is admissible only if the *Miranda* error was made in good faith.

   (b)   Police may not in bad faith obtain an unlawful confession, then read the defendant his *Miranda* rights, obtain a lawful confession, and then offer the lawful confession as fruit of the poisonous tree.

5.9 The Right to Counsel in Interrogations

5.9.1   Under the Sixth Amendment Right to Counsel, defendants have a right to an attorney **after adversarial proceedings** have begun—when the defendant is formally charged with an offense.

5.9.2   Thus, pre-indictment interrogations are generally not protected under the Sixth Amendment. *Massiah v. United States* (U.S. 1964) (Stewart, J.). The Court held that the right to counsel does not apply in *Escobedo v. Illinois* (U.S. 1964).

5.9.3   However, this was overruled by *Miranda v. Arizona* (U.S. 1966), and *Kirby v. Illinois* (U.S. 1972) restated the *Miranda* holding that the Sixth Amendment right to counsel applies **after "adversary judicial criminal proceedings"** have begun. This includes the indictment.

5.9.4 The doctrine was expanded in *Brewer v. Williams* (U.S. 1977), where the Court held that a defendant's Sixth Amendment Right to Counsel applies **whenever judicial proceedings are initiated against him,** even if this occurs before indictment by a preliminary hearing, arraignment, etc.

5.10 The Requirement to Testify if Offered Immunity

5.10.1 The defendant is required to testify if offered either of the following forms of immunity:

    (a) Transactional immunity

        (i) Broad, full immunity for a specific crime.

        (ii) The defendant is assured that he won't be prosecuted for **any transaction** implicated by the compelled testimony.

    (b) Use/derivative-use immunity

        (i) A narrower form of immunity.

        (ii) The defendant is assured that **his testimony and evidence deriving from it** will not be used against him in a future prosecution.

        (iii) However, the defendant may be prosecuted using outside, independent evidence.

5.10.2 The Fifth Amendment requires at least use immunity when compelling a witness to testify against himself.

5.10.3 When use immunity is offered, the Fifth Amendment Privilege against Self-Incrimination is not offended and the defendant cannot turn it down. The prosecution may, but is not required to, offer broad transactional immunity. *Kastigar v. United States* (U.S. 1972).

5.11 Invocation and Waiver of the *Miranda* Rights

5.11.1 The Requirement that Waivers Be Voluntary, Knowing, and Intelligent

    (a) A defendant may waive his *Miranda* rights, provided that the waiver is **voluntary, knowing, and intelligent,** which the prosecution has the "heavy burden" of proving.

    (b) Waiving the Right to Remain Silent

        (i) If the defendant talks, he waives the right to remain silent.

        (ii) If the defendant does not affirmatively invoke the right and remains silent, *the right is not waived.*

            (1) Example: police take the defendant into custody where they read him his *Miranda* rights. The defendant says nothing. Police proceed to interrogate him and the defendant confesses. Has the defendant waived his rights?

            (2) No; the waiver *may not be presumed* by the defendant's silence.

(iii) If the defendant waives the Fifth Amendment privilege against self-incrimination as to a subject matter, **he waives it as to issues of the whole crime charged.** However, the defendant may not be interrogated as to other, unrelated crimes.

5.11.2 Waiver Following Invocation

(a) If police read the defendant his *Miranda* rights and the defendant decides to exercise his rights and not to speak, the police may later return to him after a reasonable time has passed, reread his rights, and try to interrogate him anew. *Michigan v. Mosley* (U.S. 1975).

(b) However, multiple interrogations may get to the point of harassing the defendant into confessing. This is impermissible.

(c) Furthermore, *Miranda* Rights are offense-specific. Police may ask the defendant about one crime, and if the defendant refuses to speak, they can read the defendant's rights afresh for another offense and resume interrogation. The defendant may selectively waive some of his rights..

(d) Compare the right to counsel, which is not offense-specific. Once the defendant invokes his right to counsel, police must stop interrogation about *any* crime.

(i) *See Edwards v. Arizona* (U.S. 1981) by Justice White, where the defendant invoked his right to counsel and police stopped asking questions, but the next morning, resumed questioning him. Held: the right to counsel is different from the right to remain silent. Remaining silent is clear to the average person knowing his interests. But asking for a lawyer means that the defendant does not know what is in his best interests. Thus, once the defendant asks for counsel, police must stop questioning until the defendant has the opportunity to confer with a lawyer.

(e) The defendant's Right to Counsel is not offended, however, if he changes his mind and later initiates the contact.

(f) Thus, even if the defendant invokes the right against self-incrimination, police may later interrogate him, with or without rereading him his *Miranda* rights. Police may not, however, interrogate the defendant once he invokes his right to counsel, unless the defendant voluntarily initiates the communication.

5.11.3 Invocation of the Right to Counsel

(a) The right to counsel is invoked only if the defendant **clearly and unequivocally** requests counsel. *Davis v. United States* (U.S. 1994).

(b) The fact finder must find clear evidence that the defendant is asserting a constitutional right. Otherwise, police should not be penalized for asking the defendant questions.

(c) Examples:

(i) "I want a lawyer" → clear invocation meeting the test.

(ii) "Maybe I should talk to a lawyer" → does not meet the test.

5.11.4 Implied Waiver

(a) A waiver may be express (*e.g.*, through the signing of a waiver form; through the statement, "I waive my rights") or implied.

(b) When the defendant is aware of his rights but elects to talk anyway, his rights are impliedly waived, *even if he refuses to sign a written waiver form. North Carolina v. Butler* (U.S. 1979) (Stewart, J.).

(c) A waiver does not need to be absolute in order to be valid; it may be partial.

(d) However, silence does not imply a waiver of the Privilege against Self-Incrimination. The rights are still present, even if the defendant does not affirmatively invoke them. Although they can be affirmatively waived expressly or impliedly, they cannot be waived by silence.

   (i) Compare the Right to Counsel, which is waived if not affirmatively invoked.

5.11.5 *Miranda* Summary

(a) Statements made while not in custody are admissible for any purpose.

   (i) However, even these statements must be made voluntarily, since involuntary statements are *never admissible*.

   (ii) Custodial statements in violation of *Miranda* are admissible for impeachment purposes if they are voluntary.

(b) Custodial statements are admissible for any purpose if there is a valid waiver of rights.

   (i) Custodial interrogation may not begin until there has been an affirmative waiver of rights and may continue until there has been an unequivocal exercise of rights.

   (ii) The waiver is not presumed by silence (however, the right to counsel must be affirmatively invoked).

   (iii) If the defendant waives the right, he may revoke it at anytime. Police are then required to immediately stop.

6 Fifth Amendment Grand Juries, Due Process, and Charging

6.1 Grand Jury Indictments

6.1.1 Grand juries are investigative bodies with the power to issue subpoenas and grant immunity.

6.1.2 The proceedings of grand juries are held in secret, unless the court orders that grand jury transcripts be unsealed (*e.g.*, to impeach a witness who testifies differently in the trial).

6.1.3 The Fifth Amendment requires grand jury indictments in federal court ("[n]o person shall be held to answer for a capital, or otherwise infamous crime, unless on a presentment or indictment of a Grand Jury").

6.1.4 However, the Fifth Amendment Grand Jury Clause has not been incorporated against the states. The states are therefore not required to indict defendants through grand juries.[3]

6.2 Charging, Due Process and Equal Protection

6.2.1 Introduction

    (a) The Fourteenth Amendment Equal Protection Clause and the Due Process Clause of the Fifth and Fourteenth Amendments may be violated by the manner in which a prosecutor decides to bring a charge.

    (b) For example, the **Equal Protection Clause** would be violated if a prosecutor singles out one particular racial for a crime that is committed by a much wider group.

    (c) **Due Process** would be violated if the prosecutor charges a defendant in response to the defendant's exercising of some constitutional right.

6.2.2 Due Process and Vindictive Prosecutions

    (a) The Due Process Clauses does not permit prosecutors to vindictively punish defendants for exercising a statutory right to appeal.

        (i) *See North Carolina v. Pearce* (U.S. 1969) (Stewart, J.), where the defendant was originally charged with a felony and under a plea bargain, pled guilty to a misdemeanor, but later appealed. The prosecutor was indignant and reacted by re-indicting him for the felony. Held: the prosecutor punished the defendant for exercising his statutory right to appeal. If the prosecutor had put into the agreement that the defendant would not appeal, he would have avoided this problem. Reversed.

    (b) However, when two statutes overlap, the prosecutor may in his discretion charge the defendant with the statute carrying the greater penalty. *United States v. Batchelder* (U.S. 1979) (Marshall, J.). Such a charge is not considered to be vindictive.

6.2.3 Equal Protection

    (a) When bringing charges, prosecutors may not single out and prosecute groups for reasons other than their participation in a crime; as doing so would violate the equal protection of citizens under the law. *See Yick Wo v. Hopkins* (U.S. 1886) (Mathews, J.).

    (b) There is a three-part test for determining when enforcement violates equal protection. The burden is on the defendant to show the following:

        (i) There is a failure to prosecute others similarly situated;

        (ii) The failure is intentional and not accidental or inadvertent; and

        (iii) There is an arbitrary (rather than a rational) reason for the discrimination. *Oyler v. Boles* (U.S. 1962).

---

[3] Most states charge the defendant using an "information," which is a written accusation presented by a public official (as opposed to a grand jury), on his oath. Some states, such as Virginia, nevertheless require indictments by grand juries.

(c) Discrimination in the Composition of the Grand Jury

    (i) Grand jurors are summoned from community to investigate using summons, etc., returning bills of indictment if their investigation concludes with probable cause to show the defendant is guilty.

    (ii) If the composition of a grand jury is tainted by discrimination, the indictment is invalid and a new one is required.

        (1) In *Campbell v. Louisiana* (U.S. 1998), Justice Kennedy restated a former case holding that grand juries may not be discriminated against on the basis of race. When the grand jury is tainted by discrimination, the defendant suffers in fact. Louisiana argued that this should not matter: if the defendant was convicted, it doesn't matter whether the charging document was defective, since the jury was told not to consider the indictment. Held: this argument is rejected. Discrimination strikes at the fundamental trust in our jury system. This discrimination undermines confidence in our system and a new indictment is required. The original charge is constitutionally void.

7 Sixth Amendment Trial Rights

7.1 Introduction to the Sixth Amendment

7.1.1 The Sixth Amendment establishes rights that apply to both the trial and to pre-trial proceedings.

7.1.2 It establishes that, "In all criminal prosecutions, the accused shall enjoy the right to a speedy and public trial, by an impartial jury of the state and district wherein the crime shall have been committed, which district shall have been previously ascertained by law, and to be informed of the nature and cause of the accusation; to be confronted with the witnesses against him; to have compulsory process for obtaining witnesses in his favor, and to have the Assistance of Counsel for his defence."

7.1.3 It protects the rights to the following:

    (a) A speedy trial;

    (b) A public trial;

    (c) An impartial jury;

    (d) Confront one's accusers; and

    (e) The assistance of counsel.

7.2 The Right to a Speedy Trial

7.2.1 The Sixth Amendment provides that in "all criminal prosecutions, the accused shall enjoy **the right to a speedy and public trial**."

7.2.2 The Sixth Amendment protects the right to a *speedy trial*, not the right to a *speedy charge*. Thus, the clock does not begin ticking *until the defendant is actually charged* (post-accusation rule). *United States v. Marion* (U.S. 1971) (White, J.).

(a) However, Fourteenth Amendment Due Process is violated if the government's delay in filing charges is **deliberate**, done in **bad faith** or with an **improper purpose**, such as gaining a technical advantage over the accused.

(b) However, when the delay is due to the prosecution's completion of a thorough and proper investigation, there is no Due Process violation, even if the delay in some ways prejudices the defense.

(i) See *United States v. Lovasco* (U.S. 1977) (Marshall, J.), where before the indictment, two witnesses in the defendant's favor died. The defendant raised a novel due process argument: the eighteen month delay in indicting him violated his Fourteenth Amendment Due Process rights because he was prejudiced by the death of the two witnesses. Held: there is no violation of Due Process, since the apparent reason for the delay was a desire to obtain more evidence, which furthers an important government interest.

7.2.3 Once the defendant is indicted, if his right to a speedy trial is violated, the remedy is dismissal.

7.2.4 The defendant may waive the right to a speedy trial by his conduct (*e.g.*, by not raising this defense in a timely manner). See *Doggett v. United States* (U.S. 1992) (Souter, J.).

7.2.5 How Speedy is a Speedy Trial?

(a) Determining whether a trial was speedy involves a totality of the circumstances analysis that looks to factors such as whether the defendant was causing delays.

(b) Many states have also adopted speedy trial statutes. For example, Virginia requires triales within five months when the defendant is in custody and nine months when he is on bond.

7.3 The Right to a Fair Trial, the Press, and Publicity

7.3.1 The right to a public trial guarantees that the defendant's substantive and procedural due process rights can be scrutinized out in the open before the public and the press.

7.3.2 Any scandalous or corrupt acts will quickly be brought to light.

7.3.3 However, there are times when a public trial will actually act to the *detriment* of the defendant, as when, in a notorious case, the entire community is made aware of a case before a jury is even impaneled.

7.3.4 In such situations, where a pre-trial suppression hearing of a confession or an illegal seizure is made known to the public at large, the chances of impaneling an *impartial jury* will be substantially compromised.

7.3.5 The normally symbiotic relationship between the defendant's right to a public trial and the press's rights to free speech can be turned into a relationship of conflict.

7.3.6 The courts can sometimes resolve the tension through the sequestration of the jury and instructions that jury members not to speak to *anyone* outside of the court about the case.

7.3.7 Sometimes, however, such remedies will be inadequate. For example, if the defendant waives his right to a public trial, his waiver will enter into conflict with the First Amendment interests of the press.

7.3.8   The court will be forced into balancing the rights of one against the other in order to determine which one prevails.

7.3.9   The court will close the trial to the press and to the general public only under the following conditions:

   (a)   The state shows an *overwhelming interest* (*e.g.*, the need to protect a witness);

   (b)   The closure is *no broader than necessary* to further that interest;

   (c)   The court must consider *reasonable alternatives* (jury instructions, sequestration of the jury, etc.); and

   (d)   The court makes *findings on the record* adequate to support whatever decision it makes. *Waller v. Georgia* (U.S. 1984).

7.3.10 The court may find that the defendant's right to a future jury untainted by news from a preliminary hearing trumps the press's First Amendment rights. In such cases, it may enjoin the press from covering the hearing.

   (a)   *See Gannett Co., Inc. v. DePasquale* (U.S. 1979), where the defendant moved to suppress a confession and to exclude the media and public from the suppression hearing in order to prevent the media from finding out what he had said in the confession. Both parties agreed, but the press filed a writ of *mandamus* asserting a First Amendment right to hear it. Held: the defendant's right to a fair trial outweighs the freedom of the press. The Sixth Amendment **right to a public trial is for the benefit of the defendant,** not of the press. The Constitution mentions not the right of the public to a fair trial, but of the accused to a public trial. Furthermore, there is a difference between a trial and a pre-trial hearing; the requirement of a public trial does not apply pre-trial, as in this case. Here, the judge was taking steps with the agreement of the parties to minimize the risks of having a future jury tainted. The public's right of access does not necessarily apply to pre-trial hearings.

7.3.11 *Richmond Newspapers, Inc. v. Virginia* (U.S. 1980) discussed the need to balance the Sixth Amendment right to a public trial, which the defendant can waive, and First Amendment freedoms, but it gave little guidance.

7.3.12 The Sixth Amendment right to an impartial jury (which is intimately tied to the right to a public trial) does not require that a jury completely ignorant of the facts of the case be impanelled.

7.3.13 It requires simply that jurors be able to lay aside impressions acquired from pre-trial publicity in order to be able to give a verdict based only on that which is presented in the courtroom.

   (a)   *See Irvin v. Dowd* (U.S. 1961) (Clark, J.), where several egregious murders by a serial killer in 1954-55 created a great deal of publicity. When the prosecutor gave a press release stating that the defendant had confessed to all six murders, the widwspread publicity led the defendant sought a change of venue, which was granted in the adjoining county. The defendant moved for a change of venue outside of the media market, which was denied, and he was convicted. Held: in these days of swift communication, it is neither possible nor expected that jurors will be totally ignorant of the facts of a case. It is sufficient only that **jurors be able to lay aside impressions and give a verdict based on only what they learn in the courtroom.** Here, however, the prejudice was too strong, since the record shows that each juror knew that the defendant had already confessed. It would be very difficult to purge this from the jurors' minds. The refusal to allow a change of venue compromised the right to a fair trial.

7.3.14 When the press causes enough commotion to effect a probability of unfairness, the Fourteenth Amendment Due Process Clause becomes implicated.

(a) See *Sheppard v. Maxwell* (U.S. 1966) (Clark, J.), where a great deal of media attention was generated at the murder of the wife of the defendant, a doctor. The press immediately accused the defendant, with one front page story, among others, stating, "Why isn't Sam Sheppard in Jail?" The defendant was convicted and appealed on the basis of his due process rights. Held: the defendant **was denied his Fourteenth Amendment Due Process rights** when reporters took over the courtroom and hounded him. Twenty reporters were taking notes within the bar throughout the trial. The judge, assigning the places to the reporters, caused confusion and commotion that had a negative impact on the fairness of the trial, as it did here. There *must be a new trial*.

7.4 The Right to a Trial by an Impartial Jury

7.4.1 The Sixth Amendment provides that "[i]n all criminal prosecutions, the accused shall enjoy the right to a speedy and public trial, **by an impartial jury** of the state and district wherein the crime shall have been committed . . ."

7.4.2 A defendant has a right to a trial by jury whenever he is charged with a *crime*, which, unlike a *petty offense*, is any charge that carried **more than a six month jail term**.

7.4.3 Thus, if *criminal imprisonment* for **more than six months** is possible, the state must provide the right to a trial by jury. *Baldwin v. New York* (U.S. 1970).

7.4.4 This constitutional requirement trumps any conflicting state constitutional provisions.

(a) See *Duncan v. Louisiana* (U.S. 1968) (White, J.), where the Court held that the Louisiana Constitution is subject to the Impartial Jury Clause of the Constitution. It is not relevant that Lousiana's legal system derived from the French civil law; once it joined the union, it was requird to conform to the federal Constitution.

7.4.5 The Constitution does not always require twelve jurors—this is just a "historical accident."

7.4.6 Many scholars believe that where there is a capital case, twelve jurors is required. However, as the law stands, six would be sufficient.

7.4.7 Unanimity among the jurors is not required by the Constitution. The Court has held that a ten-two supermajority is acceptable; in another case, a nine-three supermajority was permitted. However, most states require unanimous verdicts.

7.4.8 However, if there is a jury of less than twelve, a unanimous verdict is necessary whenever the defendant is charged with more than a petty offense.

7.4.9 The selection process must be about being fair and impartial and must not exclude anyone based on some improper motivation.

7.4.10 Lawyers may inquire as to the views of potential jurors on the issues of the case.

(a) *See Witherspoon v. Illinois* (U.S. 1968) (Stewart, J.), where the jurors were asked whether they were opposed to the death penalty. The prosecutor objected to the question and the judge allowed just the question with no further questioning. Held: the trial court erred because both the prosecution and the defense must be permitted to inquire jurors of their positions of issues "inextricably entwined" in the case in order to *unveil bias*. However, a lawyer may not automatically disqualify a juror unless it is clear that the juror is unable to render a fair verdict (*e.g.*, the juror states that under no circumstances will he be able to follow the law because he opposes capital punishment).

7.4.11 A fair cross section is a constitutional requirement guaranteed by the Sixth Amendment. *Taylor v. Louisiana* (U.S. 1975) (White, J.).

7.4.12 However, this does not necessarily mean that the defendant is entitled to a jury with an *exact representation* of the demographics of the community.

7.5 The Right to a Fair Trial: Jury Selection

7.5.1 *Voir dire* is the process in which attorneys examine prospective jurors to determine competency and potential bias. The process leads to the rejection or selection of those who will ultimately serve on the jury.

7.5.2 Peremptory challenges allow the parties to exclude prospective jurors from the jury without having to give a reason.

7.5.3 Peremptory challenges based on race alone are prohibited by the Equal Protection Clause.

7.5.4 A defendant who challenges a peremptory challenge on this basis has the burden of:

(a) Proving that he is a **member of a protected class;**

(b) Making a *prima facie* showing that the prosecution has used peremptory challenges to **systematically exclude jurors** who are members of that protected class[4]; and

(c) Once these two prongs are met, an *inference is raised* that the prosecution's exclusion of jurors was based on race and the *burden then shifts to the prosecutor* to provide a neutral explanation for the exclusion based on something other than membership in the protected class. *Batson v. Kentucky* (U.S. 1986) (Powell, J.).

7.5.5 The Court has held that gender is a protected class, *J.E.B. v. Alabama* (U.S. 1994) (Blackmun, J.), and some scholars argue that religion is one as well.

7.5.6 In *Holland v. Illinois* (U.S. 1990) (Scalia, J.), the Court held that it has been going about this in the wrong way by focusing on the Sixth Amendment right to an impartial jury. Rather, the Fourteenth Amendment Due Process rights of jurors justify the *Batson v. Kentucky* and *J.E.B. v. Alabama* holdings. The jurors have a right to serve and the parties represent the jurors' interests.

(a) When the prosecution systematically excludes minorities from the jury, it is not the defendant's Sixth Amendment right to a fair trial that is offended, but rather, the juror's Due Process rights.

---

[4] This showing can be established solely on the prosecution's use of race in the defendant's trial in excluding jurors.

(b) Therefore, the criminal defendant is not the only party that has a right to challenge the exclusion of jurors; the prosecution may also challenge the defendant's exclusion of jurors based on the same Due Process rights of the jurors.

(c) Furthermore, since the right is rooted in the Fourteenth Amendment Due Process Clause, it applies not only in criminal cases, but in *civil cases* as well.

7.5.7 In *Johnson v. California* (U.S. 2005) (Stevens, J.), the *Batson* analysis changed and challenging a peremptory challenge requires two steps only:

(a) The defendant must make a *prima facie* showing that the prosecution has used peremptory challenges to **systematically exclude jurors** based on their membership of that protected class; and

(b) If the trial judge is satisfied that that is the case, **the burden shifts to the prosecutor** to provide a **neutral explanation** for the exclusion based on something other than membership in the protected class.

(c) Example:

(i) The prosecutor strikes three Hispanic Americans from the jury. The defendant argues that the prosecutor is excluding jurors based on their membership in a protected class. If the court holds that it is not satisfied that the prosecution is doing this, then that is the end of the analysis.

(ii) If, however, the court is satisfied that the prosecutor is using his peremptory challenges in a discriminatory manner, then the prosecutor must provide a neutral explanation.

(iii) If the prosecutor admits that he is discriminating based on race, then the excluded juror is brought back in.

(iv) If, however, he gives a neutral reason for the exclusion and the judge is convinced that those are the actual reasons, then the *Batson* challenge fails.

(d) The standard of review on appeal is abuse of discretion. If there is any evidence to sustain the trial court's decision, it will stand.

7.6 The Right to a Fair Trial: Exculpatory Evidence

7.6.1 Exculpatory evidence is evidence that tends to clear the defendant from criminal liability by, for example, proving his innocence, proving his guilt for a lesser crime, or mitigating his punishment.

7.6.2 Due process requires that prosecutors turn over all **material** exculpatory evidence to the defendant.

(a) *See Brady v. Maryland* (U.S. 1963) (Douglas, J.), where the witness gave a different statement in court than that given previously to law enforcement. The defendant asked for the statements that the witnesses made to police, but the prosecutor refused to disclose them. Held: due process requires the prosecutor to **reveal material exculpatory evidence** when requested by the defendant. Here, the prosecution failed to turn over material statements. Reversed.

7.6.3 However, when the exculpatory evidence is not material, the prosecutor will not be required to turn it over to the defense.

(a) *See United States v. Agurs* (U.S. 1976) (Stevens, J.), where although the defendant asked the prosecutor for any evidence that could have exculpated him, information that could have impacted a witness's credibility was not turned over. The lower courts overturned the conviction based on *Brady*. Held: the exculpatory information must be *material;* here, it was not. Furthermore, in *Brady*, we said that it is error for the prosecutor not to turn over exculpatory evidence when the defendant makes a *specific* request. Here, there was only a *general request, which is the functional equivalent of no request* at all.

7.6.4 If a *general request* or *no request* for exculpatory evidence is made, the prosecutor must turn over any material exculpatory information he may have.

7.6.5 If a *specific request* for material exculpatory information is made, the prosecutor must either:

(a) Turn over the requested information; or

(b) Let the judge review the record *in camera* if he disputes having exculpatory evidence. *United States v. Agurs* (U.S. 1976).

7.6.6 Defining the "Material" Element

(a) In *United States v. Bagley* (U.S. 1985), the Court held that evidence is "material" if there is a "*reasonable probability*" that had it been disclosed, the trial would have had a *different outcome*.

(b) Later, the Court refined this definition and held that the prosecution must turn over any evidence when there is a *reasonable probability* that it would be **material to the defense**. There are four aspects of the reasonable probability:

(i) It requires not a preponderance of the evidence, but rather, a **reasonable probability**;

(ii) It does not require that the defendant show that he **could not be convicted without the evidence**;

(iii) If a defendant has demonstrated a reasonable probability of the outcome, the court cannot find that the withholding did not cause injury (*the error may not be held harmless*); and

(iv) While the prosecutor is not required to show everything helpful to the defense, he must **gauge the net effect** and disclose when reasonable probability is reached. *Kyles v. Whitely* (U.S. 1995).

(c) When evidence that had a reasonable probability of being material to the defense is excluded, the defendant is entitled to a new trial.

7.7 The Right to a Fair Trial: an Impartial Judge

7.7.1 The Sixth Amendment guarantees the **right to an impartial judge** as part of a fair trial through the Due Process Clauses of the Fifth and Fourteenth Amendments.

7.7.2 The judge must be neutral and detached—he may be neither financially nor otherwise connected to the outcome of the case.

    (a)   *See Ward v. City of Monroeville* (U.S. 1972) (Brennan, J.), where the defendant was convicted of two traffic violations under an Ohio statute that allowed mayors to sit as judges in traffic offenses. Held: there is an *appearance of impropriety* and a *conflict of interest* because the mayor indirectly benefits every time somebody is convicted, since fines contribute to the town treasury. The right to an impartial judge has been violated.

7.7.3 Pre-Trial Rights

    (a)   The right to an impartial judge similarly applies before the actual trial: the custody and bail decision must be made before a neutral, detached judicial officer.

    (b)   In order to detain a defendant before trial, there must be a *Gerstein* hearing before a *neutral magistrate* to determine probable cause.

        (i)   *See Gerstein v. Pugh* (U.S. 1975), holding that when a person is arrested with no warrant or indictment, he is entitled to a hearing by a *neutral magistrate* to determine probable cause. The hearing should take place promptly after the arrest in order to avoid unconstitutional restraints on liberty.

8   The Sixth Amendment Confrontation Clause

8.1   The Incidental Rights to Be Present and Informed of the Accusation

8.1.1 The Confrontation Clause is established in the Sixth Amendment, which states that in all criminal prosecutions, the accused shall enjoy the right "to be confronted with the witnesses against him."

8.1.2 This right necessarily implies the **right to be present** at one's trial, since the defendant who is not present will not have the opportunity to confront those witnesses who testify against him.

    (a)   This right is not absolute; it may be waived by the defendant's disruptive behavior in the courtroom.

    (b)   After a warning, the court may remove the defendant from the courtroom, who thereby loses his right to confront witnesses against him.

        (i)   *See Illinois v. Allen* (U.S. 1970) (Black, J.), where the defendant, who represented himself, threatened the judge and destroyed a file in the courtroom. After an initial warning, which was to no avail, the trial judge removed the defendant from the courtroom and ordered the defendant's standby counsel to be present. The defendant challenged the decision. Held: if a defendant is warned of the consequences of his conduct, he can waive his right to be present if he persists in his misconduct. If the defendant later promises to behave, he may return.

8.1.3 If the defendant has a right to be physically present in the courtroom, by corollary, he also has a right to understand and "**be informed of the nature and cause of the accusation**."[5]

---

[5] U.S. Const. amend. VI.

- (a) His presence in the courtroom is not meaningful unless he understands what is happening therein.

- (b) Due process requires that *incompetent defendants not be tried* until they regain competence (through medical treatment, theraphy, etc.).

- (c) When there is a reasonable doubt as to the defendant's competence, there is to be a competency hearing.

    - (i) *See Pate v. Robinson* (U.S. 1966) (Clark, J.), where the defendant claimed insanity and incompetence to stand trial. The state insisted that Robinson waived these rights. Held: when either party raises a *bona fide* doubt, due process requires that a hearing to determine competency be held. If an incompetent the defendant is tried, *the right to be present is rendered meaningless*.

8.2 Introduction to the Confrontation Clause

8.2.1 The Sixth Amendment Confrontation Clause gives the accused the right to confront all witnesses against him "in all criminal prosecutions."[6]

- (a) *See Griffin v. California* (U.S. 1965) (Douglas, J.), where the Court held that the Confrontation Clause would be violated if a prosecutor, on closing argument, implied that the defendant was guilty because he did not take the stand, since the prosecutor could not be cross examined.

8.2.2 The Sixth Amendment Confrontation Clause is the right to cross-examine witnesses and to test evidence being used against the defendant.

8.2.3 The right to confront is to be read in the context of the drafting of the common law at the time of the ratification of the Constitution, which is what the founders had in mind.

8.3 The History of the Confrontation Clause

8.3.1 The Court has held that, where one codefendant gives a confession implicating another, the first codefendant's confession is admissible against the second codefendant only **if the first codefendant takes the stand** and submits himself to cross-examination.

- (a) *See Bruton v. United States* (U.S. 1968) (Brennan, J.), where the prosecutor tried to convict one of the codefendants by using a statement that implicated a second codefendant. The defendant subpoenaed the second codefendant, but the second codefendant refused to testify under the Fifth Amendment, since she was on trial. Held: under these circumstances, the invocation of the Fifth Amendment made the second codefendant unavailable to the first, thereby infringing on his right to confront witnesses that testify against him. The cases can be tried separately, but this may not be practical and the courts cannot tell the Executive Branch how to bring charges.

8.3.2 Later, the Court held that the Confrontation Clause does not guarantee cross-examination, but rather, only **the opportunity to cross-examine**.

- (a) *See Ohio v. Roberts* (U.S. 1980) (Blackmun, J.), where evidence was presented at a preliminary hearing by a witness who later became unavailable. The prosecution offered the testimony of the

---

[6] U.S. Const. amend. VI.

witness from the preliminary hearing. The defendant objected on the basis of the Confrontation Clause. Held: the Confrontation Clause was not violated. At the preliminary hearing, the witness was presented and placed under oath, *but the defendant chose not to cross examine*. The Constitution guarantees only the opportunity to cross-examine. The state may therefore use the testimony in trial, even though the witness became unavailable.

    (b)   *N.B.*: this rule applies only to situations in which the witness becomes unavailable. If the witness is available, the prior testimony cannot be offered in lieu of the actual testimony.

8.3.3   In dicta, the *Ohio v. Roberts* Court held that *the FRE and the Sixth Amendment are largely congruent*. If the FRE are complied with, the Constitution is satisfied. An out of court statement against the defendant was admissible, even if the defendant did not have the opportunity to confront the witness, if it bore an **"adequate indicia of reliability."**

8.3.4   This test was met if either of the following elements was satisfied:

    (a)   The evidence fell within a "firmly rooted hearsay exception"; or

    (b)   The evidence contained "particularized guarantees of trustworthiness."

8.3.5   The *Roberts* ruling worked well until 1999, when *Lilly v. Virginia* was handed down.

    (a)   In *Lilly v. Virginia* (U.S. 1999) (Stevens, J.), three codefendants, the defendant, his brother, and his roommate, broke into a home and stole guns, liquor, and a safe. They later kidnapped a passing motorist and committed robberies and murder. All were later taken into custody and questioned. The defendant did not mention the murder and explained that his brother and roommate forced him to participate in the robberies. The others stated that the defendant masterminded the incidents. The state charged the defendant with several offenses and offered his statements as declarations against penal interest as an exception to the hearsay rule. The lower courts held that since the FRE were satisfied, the statements were admissible under *Ohio v. Roberts*. The defendant appealed. Held: because the declaration against penal interest exception to the hearsay rule does not trace its way back to the time of the *ratification of the Bill of Rights*, it is not **firmly rooted** and is not what the framers had the mind. *Ohio v. Roberts* is good law, but **in order for a FRE to be good under the Sixth Amendment, it must be firmly rooted.**

    (b)   *N.B.*: many commentators read this case as saying that a FRE must be rooted in the rules of evidence as they were at the time of the ratification.

8.4   The Confrontation Clause Today

8.4.1   Supreme Court jurisprudence based on *Roberts* was radically overturned in 2004, when the *Crawford* Court introduced the **testimonial** test:

    (a)   If the evidence is not testimonial in nature, the Constitution is not implicated; if it is, then the defendant must have the opportunity to confront his accuser.

    (b)   Evidence is testimonial when it is being used **in furtherance of criminal prosecution**.

8.4.2   Evidence obtained in a 911 call whose primary purpose is to obtain emergency assistance is not testimonial in nature. The Confrontation Clause is therefore *not implicated*.

(a) *See Crawford v. Washington* (U.S. 2004) (Scalia, J.), where Michael Crawford stabbed Keneeth Lee, who he suspected of sexually assaulting his (Crawford's) wife. During the trial, the defendant's wife did not testify because of the marital privilege, but the prosecution played a recorded statement that she previously made to police and that contradicted Crawford's claim that he acted in self-defense. Crawford challenged the recording as violative of the Confrontation Clause. The state Supreme Court upheld his conviction, relying on the "adequate indicia of reliability" test of *Ohio v. Roberts* (U.S. 1980), which permits out of court statements against a defendant when such statements are reliable. Held: *Ohio v. Roberts* is overruled. The test for determining whether the Confrontation Clause was violated is no longer whether incriminating evidence that is admitted is reliable; rather, when the defendant does not have the opportunity to confront a witness, incriminating evidence is to be excluded when it is **"testimonial" in nature**. Here, the wife's statements were testimonial and yet were admitted against the defendant, in violation of his right to confront witnesses. Judgment reversed.

    (i) *N.B.:* Justice Scalia did not explicitly define "testimonial," but he said that affidavits are testimonial, while business records are not. Some courts began to define "testimonial" as that which is prepared specifically for court (a business record would thus not qualify).

(b) *See also Davis v. Washington* (U.S. 2006) (Scalia, J.), where the defendant was charged of assaulting his wife. At trial, the prosecutor offered his wife's 911 call into evidence against the defendant, pursuant to the excited utterance exception to the hearsay rules. The defendant objected. Held: 911 calls are not testimonial, since the circumstances behind them **do not indicate that they are being used in furtherance of criminal prosecution.** Rather, they are given in the hopes of securing immediate assistance. Here, unlike in *Crawford v. Washington*, the statements were given to police for the purpose of securing assistance in an emergency, not for preserving evidence for trial.

(c) *Compare Hammon v. Indiana* (U.S. 2006) (companion case to *Davis v. Washington*), where a witness's statements were inadmissible because they were made to police after an assault was already complete. Thus, there was no conceivable purpose to the interrogation other than preparation of prosecution. The statements were therefore testimonial and offering them into evidence violated the Confrontation Clause.

8.5 Limitations

8.5.1 The Confrontation Clause does not apply before a grand jury, which does not confer to defendants a right to cross examine witnesses presented against them.[7] *Jenkins v. McKeithen* (U.S. 1969).

8.5.2 Furthermore, the Confrontation Clause does not always guarantee the right of the defendant to be **physically present** before witnesses testifying against him; other prevailing interests may apply.

(a) *See Maryland v. Craig* (U.S. 1990), where a child was permitted to testify from another room via closed circuit television. Although the defendant, an alleged sexual abuser, was unable to directly confront the child, the Confrontation Clause was not offended because the defendant was able to communicate with his attorney in real time.

---

[7] Compare with preliminary hearings, which do permit the defendant to cross-examine witnesses presented against him.

9 The Sixth Amendment Right to Counsel

9.1 Introduction

9.1.1 Until 1963, the defendant got a lawyer if he so desired, but the state was not obligated to provide one.

9.1.2 Then, in 1963, the Court held that a defendant is *always entitled to the assistance of counsel* when there is a **threat of imprisonment**, whether the prosecution is for a misdemeanor or felony.

    (a) *See Gideon v. Wainwright* (U.S. 1963) (Black, J.), where a homeless defendant handwrote a petition to the Supreme Court, explaining that he could not afford a lawyer and asked for one to be appointed. Responding to one of the most articulate writings that the Supreme Court had seen, it held that *if an offense carries the possibility of a jail sentence*, and if it is something **more than a petty offense,** the Constitution guarantees the right to an attorney of one's choosing. Otherwise, the court is to appoint an attorney of its choosing.

9.1.3 Defendants do not have a right to choose which lawyers are appointed to represent them.

    (a) *See Morris v. Slappy* (U.S. 1983), where although the defendant did not like his attorney and refused to cooperate with him, the Court refused to appoint another one.

9.1.4 The Court later extended the *Gideon* right to counsel to *any offense* where imprisonment may be imposed, whether it is a **petty offense**, a **misdemeanor**, or a **felony**. *Argersinger v. Hamlin* (U.S. 1972) (Douglas, J.).

    (a) *N.B.*: states may avoid the requirement of appointing counsel for offenses that carry jail sentences by *indicating in advance that they will ask not for imprisonment*, but rather, that only a fine be paid.

9.2 When the Right to Counsel Attaches

9.2.1 The right to counsel attaches at **all critical stages** affecting the defendant's right to a fair trial. This includes both trial and many pre-trial stages. *Massiah v. United States* (U.S. 1964); *Gilbert v. California* (U.S. 1967).

9.2.2 To qualify as a critical stage, the event must take place *after adversarial proceedings have begun*,[8] as determined from the perspective of the magistrate, such as when there is an indictment or information.

9.2.3 A critical stage is a **"trial-like event"** where the accused is confronted by a prosecutor and a procedural system where the result, without the presence of counsel, might *reduce the trial to a mere formality.*

9.2.4 **Non-critical stages** include the following:

    (a) Photographic identification proceedings. *United States v. Ash* (U.S. 1973);

    (b) Handwriting exemplar procedures. *Gilbert v. California* (U.S. 1967);

    (c) Pre-indictment police lineups. *Kirby v. Illinois* (U.S. 1972);

    (d) Detention hearings. *Gerstein v. Pugh* (U.S. 1975); and

---

[8] Adversarial proceedings are marked by lawyers and judges.

(e) The administrative detention of prison inmates. *United States v. Gouveia* (U.S. 1984).

9.2.5 **Critical stages** include the following:

(a) Police interrogations (based on the Fifth Amendment). *Miranda v. Arizona* (U.S. 1966);

(b) Preliminary hearings. *Coleman v. Alabama* (U.S. 1970)[9];

(c) Post-indictment police lineups. *United States v. Wade* (U.S. 1967);

(d) Guilty plea negotiations;

(e) Trials where imprisonment is imposed. *Argersinger v. Hamlin* (U.S. 1963); and

(f) Sentencing. *Mempa v. Rhay* (U.S. 1967).

9.3 The Right to Counsel During Identifications

9.3.1 Definitions

(a) A **showup** is where a crime has occurred and police seize a suspect, bring him to the victim, and ask the witness if that is the perpetrator. It usually occurs before an indictment when time is of the essence.

(b) A **photographic lineup** is where a witness identifies one suspect among others in a spread of photographs.

(c) A **police lineup** is where suspects are lined up at a police station.

(d) An **in-court identification** is when counsel asks a witness if she recognizes the perpetrator in court.

9.3.2 Pre-Indictment Identifications

(a) The Right to Counsel

(i) As already mentioned, the Sixth Amendment right to counsel attaches only in critical trial and pre-trial stages.

(ii) Within the context of identifications, this includes **only post-indictment identifications**. *United States v. Wade* (U.S. 1967)

(iii) There is therefore no right to counsel at a police lineup that takes place before "adversary judicial criminal proceedings" have begun. *Kirby v. Illinois* (U.S. 1972).

(b) Due Process

(i) Although the Sixth Amendment Right to Counsel does not apply to pre-indictment identifications, the Fifth Amendment Due Process Clause continues to apply.

---

[9] Preliminary hearings, which otherwise are like grand jury proceedings, permit witnesses to be cross-examined.

(ii) The defendant's due process rights do not permit the admission of unnecessarily suggestive identifications against him.

(iii) Since showups are inherently suggestive, they are admissible *only under* **exigent circumstances** (*e.g.*, the witness will die before arranging a lineup is possible) when they are **reliable** under the circumstances (not overly suggestive). *Stovall v. Denno* (U.S. 1967) (Brennan, J.).

(iv) Shifting burdens under the *Stovall* Doctrine

    (1) To exclude an identification (including a showup, a photographic lineup, or a police lineup), the defendant must meet the burden of proving that it was unreliably suggestive and unnecessary.

        (aa) Example: the defendant shows that in a photographic lineup, he was the only black suspect.

    (2) If he meets this burden, the burden of proof shifts to the prosecutor to show that under the totality of the circumstances, the identification is reliable.

    (3) Factors that the prosecutor may use to meet his burden include the accuracy of the witness's description and the time elapsed between the crime and the identification.

    (4) If the prosecutor meets his burden, the identification will be admitted. If the prosecutor fails to meet his burden, the evidence will be excluded and the witness will be prohibited from again identifying the suspect in court.

(c) Overview

(i) Thus, unlike the Sixth Amendment right to counsel, which applies only to post-indictment identifications, the *Stovall* doctrine applies to *pre-indictment identifications*.

(ii) Example: before he is indicted, the defendant is seized and brought to the victim, who is asked by police, "this is the guy, right?" Under what theory could the defendant suppress the identifation?

    (1) The Sixth Amendment is inapplicable in a pre-indictment identification.

    (2) However, under the *Stovall* Doctrine, the identification could be suppressed.

9.3.3 Post-Indictment Identifications

(a) Under the "*Wade-Gilbert* Rule," the suspect has an *absolute right* to counsel in all post-indictment critical stages, including **all post-indictment showups** and **police lineups**, but not in photographic lineups, signature analyses, and other proceedings where there is no adversarial proceeding.

(i) *See United States v. Wade* (U.S. 1967) (Brennan, J.), where the defendant was charged with bank robbery. Employees were put on stand and said that the defendant was the robber. The defendant was indicted, after which a lineup took place. Both witnesses identified the defendant in an earlier lineup. The defendant argued that his Sixth Amendment Right to Counsel was violated. Held: a post-indictment ***lineup is a critical stage*** because it is a point where the defendant *would have benefited from access to counsel*. An attorney could have advised the defendant whether or not to have participated.

(b) The purpose behind extending the right to counsel to post-indictment identifications is to protect the defendants from potential prejudicial conditions to which they may not know to object.

(c) Thus, the right to an attorney does not apply in non-adversarial proceedings because the *presence of an attorney would not help to secure the defendant's rights*.

(d) Such proceedings include handwriting analyses and photographic lineups.

    (i) *See Gilbert v. California* (U.S. 1967) (Brennan, J.) (companion case to *Wade*), where police took handwriting samples from a suspect and sent them off to a forensic lab. The defendant argued under *Wade* that he should have had an attorney present. Held: *Wade* involved a post-indictment lineup, which is a critical stage. However, ***a handwriting analysis is not a critical stage*** because the right to counsel would have been of no benefit.

    (ii) *See also United States v. Ash* (U.S. 1973), holding that the right to counsel does not extend to ***photographic lineups,*** since police may go forward with the lineup even without the defendant's participation, if they have his photograph. Even if the defendant had an attorney, he would be of no help in protecting him from prejudicial conditions.

(e) Furthermore, the "adversary judicial criminal proceedings" under *Kirby v. Illinois* (U.S. 1972) have not yet begun in pre-indictment handwriting samples and photographic lineups. Therefore, such identifications cannot be critical stages and the right to counsel is not yet activated.

9.4 Restriction on Right to Retained Counsel

9.4.1 When there are conflicts between the interests of the state and the right to retain counsel, overriding state interests may prevent defendants from asserting an absolute right to counsel.

9.4.2 For example, defendants may not hire lawyers with illegal money that rightly belongs to the state; they must pay with their own money.

(a) *See Caplin & Drysdale, Chartered v. United States* (U.S. 1989) by Justice Byron R. White, where the state sought to seize retainers paid by the defendants for their lawyers because the defendants hired their lawyers with illegal money. The overriding state interest: the money belongs to the state, which filed a forfeiture proceeding.

9.5 Right to Counsel on Appeal

9.5.1 Overview

(a) There is a right to counsel on appeal based not on the Sixth Amendment, which applies only to the trial, but on the Fourteenth Amendment Due Process Clause.

(b) This due process right to counsel requires that states provide counsel to indigents on appeal. This right applies *only to the first appeal* (due process guarantees adequate, not perfect, access to the courts). *Douglas v. California* (U.S. 1963) (Douglas, J.).

(c) Although there is no constitutional right to counsel *after the first appeal*, some states grant defendants the assistance of counsel.

9.5.2 Obligation of Counsel in Meritless Appeal

(a) Defendants have a right to appeal under *Douglas*, even if their counsel believes that there was no reversible error to appeal.

(b) If the defendant's counsel truly believes that the appeal is frivolous, he must petition for the right to withdraw.

(c) He is nonetheless obligated to file an "*Anders* brief," arguing for argument that the client wants made that might support an appeal.

(d) If the court, after reading the brief, decides that there is any merit, then it must appoint new counsel. *Anders v. California* (U.S. 1967) (Clark, J.).

9.5.3 Right to Trial Transcripts in the Appeal

(a) A defendant cannot have a meaningful appeal without the trial transcripts.

(b) If the defendant is indigent, the state must pay for the transcripts on appeal (if he is not indigent, he must pay). *Griffen v. Illinois* (U.S. 1956) (Black, J.) (*N.B.*: this was decided before *Gideon* held in 1963 that there was a right to counsel).

9.6 Right to Experts

9.6.1 Indigent defendants have a right to the "basic tools" of an adequate trial, such as the right to counsel and transcripts on appeal.

9.6.2 This right includes the right to expert witnesses paid for by the state when they are needed by indigent defendants for an effective presentation of a case during the trial.

(a) *See Ake v. Oklahoma* (U.S. 1985) (Marshall, J.), where the defendant's lawyer wanted to raise the insanity defense and thus needed an expert to testify that the defendant was not guilty by reason of insanity. In a five to four decision, Justice Marshall held that he Sixth Amendment does not provide a right to experts; it supports the right to counsel. However, the Due Process Clause of the Fourteenth Amendment supports the right. An expert was required because the defendant's insanity was a *significant factor*.

(b) *N.B.*: the Court limited this right to experts *only for the advancement of affirmative defenses*, such as insanity. Furthermore, defendants are entitled to only those experts that the court is willing to appoint, not to those experts of the defendants' choosing.

9.7 Effective Assistance of Counsel

9.7.1 The Constitution requires not merely the right to counsel, but rather, the right to the *effective* assistance of counsel.

9.7.2 In *Strickland v. Washington* (U.S. 1984), the Court set out the following standard for determining whether the assistance of counsel was effective (both elements must be met):

(a) The defendant must overcome a presumption that his attorney was competent by showing that he made errors so serious that his "representation fell below an **objective standard of reasonableness**"

(i) The defendant must thus provde that the representation did not fall within the range of competence demanded in criminal cases); and

(b) The defendant must also show that the counsel's incompetent representation prejudiced him.

(i) Standard for prejudice: whether there is a reasonable probability that, but for his attorney's unprofessional errors, **the proceeding would have turned out differently** (*i.e.*, the defendant would have been aquitted or convicted of a lesser offense).

9.7.3 Defendants rarely satisfy this test (especially the second prong).

(a) *See Strickland v. Washington* (U.S. 1984) (O'Connor, J.) where the defendant Washington planned and committed a host of crimes, including capital murder, robbery, and kidnapping. The defendant made several decisions against the advice of the public defender appointed to his case, including choosing a trial by jury (which was more likely to give the death sentence); and changing his plea to guilty to all charges (including three capital murder charges). After his attorney received the discovery, he became hopeless regarding the case, cut his efforts short by not pursuing all avenues, and did not present any evidence regarding his client's character and emotional state. In deciding whether the defendant received the effective assistance of counsel, the Court held that neither prong of the test was passed. **First prong**: although the lawyer could have done some things differently, he met the minimum requirements by advising his client (*e.g.*, not to speak to the police) and making all of the appropriate pre-trial motions. **Second prong**: the defendant, by going against his attorney's advice and confessing, made it impossible for the lawyer to defend him. The defendant could not have shown in any event how the result would have been different here.

9.7.4 Presumed Prejudice

(a) In limited circumstances, it is presumed that *no lawyer* can be effective in trial.

(b) In such circumstances, *there is no need to inquire* into the attorney's conduct at the trial.

(c) Courts will look to several factors in determining making a *per se* determination of ineffective counsel, including: (i) the time to prepare the case; (ii) the experience of the attorney; (iii) the gravity of charges; and (iv) the complexity of defenses.

(d) However, the case must pass a very high threshold in order for a court to make a *per se* determination of effective counsel. Such cases are limited to those characterized by only the most egregious circumstances.

(i) *See United States v. Cronic* (U.S. 1984) (Stevens, J.), where a young real estate lawyer trying his first case was appointed to represent the defendant. The attorney had only twenty five days to prepare his case against the government, which had years on its side. Yet despite these circumstances, this case did not pass the requisite threshold. The Court held that just because it was the attorney's first trial does not mean that the representation was ineffective. Furthermore, twenty five days is not so short that there is a presumption of ineffective assistance of counsel. Although there are some cases where prejudice can be presumed, this was not one of them.

9.8 Conflicts of Interest in Multiple Representation

9.8.1 There is a limited presumption of prejudice in cases of representation of multiple defendants by a single attorney.

9.8.2 Multiple representation may limit the ability of an attorney to act in the full interests of any single defendant, since he must balance the interests of each defendant against the interests of the defendants as a whole.

9.8.3 For example, in a gang or mafia prosecution, the government may not enter into deals with some criminals in order to convict others if the defendants are represented by the same lawyer.

9.8.4 These limitations may prejudice the interests of any single defendant, who may later move for reversal based on prejudice caused from the ineffective assistance of counsel based on the multiple representation.

9.8.5 If, however, the defendant waives his right to his own, separate attorney, there can be no later claim of ineffective assistance of counsel.

9.8.6 There is, however, no absolute right to a waiver. The court is not obligated to accept the defendant's wiaver and may even require an attorney that is representing several defendants to be removed from the case.

9.8.7 To avoid appeals based on the potential prejudice inherent in multiple representation and the limitation of its ability to enter into deals with individual defendants, the government prefers that each defendant have a separate lawyer.

(a) *See Cuyler v. Sullivan* (U.S. 1980) (Powell, J.), where the government asked the trial court to disqualify an attorney who was representing multiple defendants and to appoint multiple attorneys so that the government could separately offer them deals. Issue: is there a government interest in intervening that trumps the Sixth Amendment right to choose one's attorney? Held: there is an inherent risk of ineffective assistance of counsel in cases of multiple representation; the defendants would be entitled to a reversal in the case of prejudicial error. The trial court does not, however, have to assume that there is a conflict in the defendants' sharing the same attorney; it may assume that there is no conflict or that the defendant waived his right to have his own attorney. It is nonetheless wise to inquire if prejudice is likely to occur; otherwise, if the defendant is convicted, he may be able to appeal, claiming that his attorney did not effectively act in his interest. Thus, when the government protests multiple representations, the trial courts should ask whether the defendants understand the potential problem and waive it. If they do not, there may need to be a full retrial if the defendants show: (i) there was a conflict; and (ii) the lawyer acted adverse to their interests.

9.9 Self-Representation

9.9.1 The corollary of the right to counsel is the *right to not have counsel*. Like any constitutional rights, it may be waived.

9.9.2 The Court has characterized the waiver of counsel not as a waiver, but as a constitutional right—*i.e.*, there is an *affirmative right to self-representation* that courts must honor when invoked.

9.9.3 However, the Court treats the right as a waiver, since exercising it must be *knowing, intelligent, and voluntary*.

  (a) *See Faretta v. California* (U.S. 1975) (Stewart, J.), where the defendant was charged with murder and was facing the death penalty. The defendant said that God would be his lawyer. The judge appointed a lawyer anyway. Although the lawyer did a good job, the defendant was convicted. There was no ineffective assistance of counsel claim, but the defendant alleged that the Sixth Amendment was violated when the judge refused to allow him to represent himself. Held: *a defendant has the right to make his own defense and must suffer the consequences if his defense fails*. There is an affirmative right to self-representation, as long as the defendant's giving up his right to counsel is knowing, intelligent, and voluntary. The defendant may waive his right to counsel if the consequences are explained to him and he is competent to make the decision.

9.9.4 If the defendant invokes the right to self-representation (waives his right to counsel) and does a poor job of representing himself, he may not make a claim claim for the ineffective assistance of counsel.

REVIEW CHARTS AND SUMMARIES

WHEN CONSTITUTIONAL RIGHTS APPLY

Fifth Amendment Right to a Trial by Jury	Anytime the defendant is charged with a crime that bears the possibility of a prison sentence of six or more months.
Sixth Amendment Right to Confront One's Accusers	When incriminating testimony offered against the defendant is *testimonial* (offered and used in furtherance of criminal prosecution).
Sixth Amendment Right to Counsel	Anytime the defendant is charged with *any offense* where prison may be imposed, whether it is a petty offense, misdemeanor, or felony. The right applies to all trial and pre-trial *critical stages*, which take place after adversarial proceedings have begun.

LANDMARK CRIMINAL PROCEDURE CASES

1925 – **Carroll v. United States** – police are not required to obtain a warrant to effect a search of automobiles and other moving vehicles when they have **probable cause** that a crime is being committed, since the time required in obtaining a search would permit the mobile evidence to be lost or destroyed.

1961 – **Mapp v. Ohio** – the exclusionary rule for illegally searches and seizures applies in the states.

1963 – **Gideon v. Wainwright** – the state must provide an attorney to indigent defendants whenever there is the possibility of imprisonment.

1963 – **Wong Sun v. United States** – illegally obtained derivative evidence ("fruit of the poisonous tree") can be purged through voluntary conduct, such as a voluntary confession given after an improperly obtained confession.

1964 – **Massiah v. United States** – the right to counsel is activated at **all critical stages** of an adversarial proceeding. Cf. *Gilbert v. California*.

1966 – **Miranda v. Arizona** – (Warren, J.) police must read defendants the four warnings in interrogations of defendants in police custody. Otherwise, confessions are to be excluded.

1967 – **Gilbert v. California** – the right to counsel applies in all critical stages of an adversarial proceeding. Signature analyses are not critical stages, since the presence of an attorney would not in any way protect a defendant.

1967 – **United States v. Wade** – post-indictment police lineups are critical stages for purposes of the Sixth Amendment Right to Counsel.

1967 – **Warden v. Hayden** - when pursuing a dangerous suspect and time is of the essence, police may conduct warrantless searches. The following elements must be met: (i) there is **probable cause** (always necessary for searches and seizures); (ii) under **exigent circumstances** justifying the warrantless search; (iii) the pursuit begins from a place where the police have **a lawful right to be;** and (iv) the legal violation is **serious** enough to justify a warrantless search.

1968 – **Terry v. Ohio** – police do not need probable cause in order to effect a frisk of a defendant's body in order to assure officer safety. If police, while conducting a frisk, develop independent probable cause that a crime is being committed or that the defendant is in possession of contraband, they may search for and seize the contraband without a warrant. A police stop does not require probable cause, but rather, a reasonable and articulate suspicion that a crime is being committed.

1969 – **Chimel v. California** – police need neither a warrant nor probable cause in order to effect a search of a defendant's wingspan (the area within his immediate control) in order to assure officer protection (**search incident to lawful arrest** exception to the need for a warrant).

1970 – **Chambers v. Maroney** – once police have seized a vehicle, they are not required to obtain a search warrant. They may search it as they would have at the time that it was stopped. Rationale: (i) cars and other mobile vehicles were primarily means of transportation; (ii) they are driven in plain view; and (iii) they are subject to heavy regulation.

1971 – **Coolidge v. New Hampshire** – when the incriminating nature of evidence is immediately apparent to police while they are in a place where they have a lawful right to be, they may seize it under the plain view doctrine.

1972 – **Argersinger v. Hamlin** – the state must provide an attorney to indigent defendants whenever imprisonment is imposed, for any offense, whether it is a felony, misdemeanor, or petty.

1972 – **Kirby v. Illinois** – there is no right to counsel under the Sixth Amendment during a pre-indictment police lineup, since adversarial judicial proceedings have not yet begun.

1973 – **United States v. Ash** – photographic lineups are not critical stages for the purposes of the Sixth Amendment Right and do not require the right of counsel.

1975 – **Gerstein v. Pugh** – a person who is arrested without a warrant is entitled to a hearing to determine whether there is probable cause to arrest him.

1975 – **Michigan v. Mosley** – if police read a defendant his *Miranda* rights and the defendant refuses to speak, the police may return to the defendant and interrogate him afresh without rereading the *Miranda* rights, provided it is done within a reasonable time.

1977 – **United States v. Chadwick** – police must first apply for a search warrant for small closed objects seized from a car before opening them. Since police may seize the objects before applying for a search warrant, the exigent circumstances inherent in mobile automobiles does not apply.

1980 – **Ohio v. Roberts** – when evidence is firmly rooted in exceptions at the time of ratification of the Constitution, it bears an adequate indicia of reliability and is not to be excluded by the Confrontation Clause. In dicta: the Confrontation Clause and the Federal Rules of Evidence are largely congruent: testimony that satisfies the rules of evidence is admissible under the Confrontation Clause.

1980 – **Rhode Island v. Innis** – courts are not required to suppress statements volunteered to the police or that are not responsive to a question, even when the *Miranda* warnings are not read.

1982 – **United States v. Ross** – when police have probable cause, they may search the entire vehicle until they find the object of the probable cause.

1984 – **Nix v. Williams** – evidence obtained through an illegal confession is not to be excluded when it would have been **inevitably discovered.**

1984 – **Berkemer v. McCarty** – a person is in police custody when he believes that he is not free to leave from the perspective of the reasonable person (objective) in his situation (subjective).

1985 – **United States v. Montoya de Hernandez** – although probable cause is generally required for all Fourth Amendment Searches and Seizures, it is not required for border searches.

2000 – **United States v. Dickerson** – (Rehnquist, C.J.) since the states and Congress have not come up with an adequate alternative to *Miranda*, the *Miranda* rule is Constitutional.

2004 – **Crawford v. Washington** – statements offered in court must be **testimonial** in order to trigger the Confrontation Clause protections.

TABLE OF CASES

Cases

Aguilar v. Texas, 378 U.S. 108 (1964), 17

Ake v. Oklahoma, 470 U.S. 68 (1985), 60

Anders v. California, 386 U.S. 738 (1967), 60

Argersinger v. Hamlin, 407 U.S. 25 (1972), 56, 57, 65

Arizona v. Fulminante, 499 U.S. 279 (1991), 39

Arizona v. Hicks, 480 U.S. 321 (1987), 23

Baldwin v. New York, 399 U.S. 66 (1970), 48

Bartkus v. Illinois, 359 U.S. 121 (1959), 31

Batson v. Kentucky, 476 U.S. 79 (1986), 49

Berkemer v. McCarty, 468 U.S. 420 (1984), 36, 66

Blockburger v. United States, 284 U.S. 299 (1932), 30, 31

Boyd v. United States, 116 U.S. 616, 6 S.Ct. 524 (1886), 10, 35

Brady v. Corbin, 495 U.S. 508 (1990), 31

Brady v. Maryland, 373 U.S. 83 (1963), 50

Braswell v. United States, 487 U.S. 99 (1988), 34

Breithaupt v. Abram, 352 U.S. 432 (1957), 22

Brewer v. Williams, 430 U.S. 387 (1977), 41

Brown v. Illinois, 422 U.S. 590 (1975), 13

Brown v. Mississippi, 297 U.S. 278 (1936), 36

Bruton v. United States, 391 U.S. 123 (1968), 53

Burks v. United States, 437 U.S. 1 (1978), 32

Cady v. Dombrowski, 413 U.S. 433 (1973), 27

California v. Hodari D., 499 U.S. 621 (1991), 15, 24

Camara v. Municipal Court, 387 U.S. 523 (1967), 26

Campbell v. Louisiana, 523 U.S. 392 (1998), 45

Caplin & Drysdale, Chartered v. United States, 491 U.S. 617 (1989), 59

Carroll v. United States, 267 U.S. 132 (1925), 20, 64

Chambers v. Maroney, 399 U.S. 42 (1970), 20, 65

Chapman v. California, 386 U.S. 18 (1967), 33

Chimel v. California, 395 U.S. 752 (1969), 20, 65

Coleman v. Alabama, 399 U.S. 1 (1970), 57

Colorado v. Connelly, 479 U.S. 157 (1986), 37

Coolidge v. New Hampshire, 403 U.S. 443 (1971), 17, 23, 65

Crawford v. Washington, 541 U.S. 36 (2004), 55, 66

Crist v. Betz, 437 U.S. 28 (1978), 28

Cuyler v. Sullivan, 446 U.S. 335 (1980), 62

Davis v. United States, 512 U.S. 452 (1994), 42

Davis v. Washington, 547 U.S. 813 (2006), 55

Doggett v. United States, 505 U.S. 647 (1992), 46

Douglas v. California, 372 U.S. 353 (1963), 60

Dunaway v. New York, 442 U.S. 200 (1979), 13, 14

Duncan v. Louisiana, 391 U.S. 145 (1968), 48

Edwards v. Arizona, 451 U.S. 477 (1981), 42

Escobedo v. Illinois, 378 U.S. 478 (1964), 40

Faretta v. California, 422 U.S. 806 (1975), 63

Fisher v. United States, 425 U.S. 391 (1976), 35

Florida v. Jimeno, 500 U.S. 248 (1991), 25

Franks v. Delaware, 438 U.S. 154 (1978), 18

Frazier v. Cupp, 394 U.S. 731 (1969), 35

Gannett Co., Inc. v. DePasquale, 443 U.S. 368 (1979), 47

Gerstein v. Pugh, 420 U.S. 103 (1975), 52, 56, 65

Gideon v. Wainwright, 372 U.S. 335 (1963), 56, 60, 64

Gilbert v. California, 388 U.S. 263 (1967), 56, 59, 64

Green v. United States, 355 U.S. 184 (1957), 32

Griffen v. Illinois, 351 U.S. 12 (1956), 60

Griffin v. California, 380 U.S. 609 (1965), 35

Groh v. Ramirez, 540 U.S. 551 (2004), 16

Hammon v. Indiana, 05-5705 547 U.S. __ (2006), 55

Harris v. New York, 401 U.S. 222 (1971), 39

Heath v. Alabama, 474 U.S. 82 (1985), 31

Henry v. United States, 361 U.S. 98 (1959), 15

Hester v. United States, 265 U.S. 57 (1924), 14

Hiibel v. Sixth Judicial District Court of Nevada, 542 U.S. 177 (2004), 33

Hoffa v. United States, 385 U.S. 293 (1966), 34

Holland v. Illinois, 493 U.S. 474 (1990), 49

Hudson v. Michigan, 547 U.S. 586 (2006), 19

Hudson v. United States, 522 U.S. 93 (1997), 28

Illinois v. Allen, 397 U.S. 337 (1970), 52

Illinois v. Caballes, 543 U.S. 405 (2005), 12

Illinois v. Gates, 462 U.S. 213 (1983), 18, 19

Illinois v. Perkins, 496 U.S. 292 (1990), 37

Illinois v. Somerville, 410 U.S. 458 (1973), 29

Irvin v. Dowd, 366 U.S. 717 (1961), 47

J.E.B. v. Alabama, 511 U.S. 127, 49

J.E.B. v. Alabama, 511 U.S. 127 (1994), 49

Jenkins v. McKeithen, 395 U.S. 411 (1969), 55

Johnson v. California, 543 U.S. 499 (2005), 50

Jones v. United States, 362 U.S. 257 (1960), 13

Kastigar v. United States, 406 U.S. 441 (1972), 41

Katz v. United States, 389 U.S. 347 (1967), 13, 14

Kirby v. Illinois, 406 U.S. 682 (1972), 40, 56, 57, 59, 65

Knowles v. Iowa, 525 U.S. 113 (1998), 20

Kotteakos v. United States, 328 U.S. 750 (1946), 33

Kyles v. Whitely, 514 U.S. 419 (1995), 51

Kyllo v. United States, 533 U.S. 27 (2001), 12

Lefkowitz v. Turley, 414 U.S. 70 (1973), 34

Lilly v. Virginia, 527 U.S. 116 (1999), 54

Linkletter v. Walker, 381 U.S. 618 (1965), 33

Lo-Ji Sales Inc. v. New York, 442 U.S. 319 (1979), 17

Mallory v. United States, 354 U.S. 449 (1957), 38

Mapp v. Ohio, 11

Maryland v. Buie, 494 U.S. 325 (1990), 20

Maryland v. Craig, 497 U.S. 836 (1990), 55

Maryland v. Pringle, 540 U.S. 366 (2003), 15

Maryland v. Wilson, 519 U.S. 408 (1997), 25

Massiah v. United States, 377 U.S. 201 (1964), 40, 56, 64

McNabb v. United States, 318 U.S. 332 (1943), 38

Mempa v. Rhay, 389 U.S. 128 (1967), 57

Michigan v. Mosley, 423 U.S. 96 (1975), 42, 65

Michigan v. Tyler, 436 U.S. 499, 21

Mincey v. Arizona, 437 U.S. 385 (1978), 19, 21

Miranda v. Arizona, 384 U.S. 436 (1966), 35, 38, 39, 40, 57, 64

Missouri v. Hunter, 459 U.S. 359 (1983), 31

Missouri v. Seibert, 124 S.Ct. 2601 (2004), 40

Morris v. Slappy, 461 U.S. 1 (1983), 56

New Jersey v. T.L.O., 469 U.S. 325 (1985), 26

New York v. Quarles, 467 U.S. 649 (1984), 39

Nix v. Williams, 467 U.S. 431 (1984), 12, 37, 65

North Carolina v. Butler, 441 U.S. 369 (1979), 43

North Carolina v. Pearce, 395 U.S. 711 (1969), 44

Ohio v. Roberts, 448 U.S. 56 (1980), 53, 54, 55, 64, 65

Oliver v. United States, 466 U.S. 170 (1984), 14

Olmstead v. United States, 277 U.S. 438 (1928), 13

Oregon v. Elstad, 470 U.S. 298 (1985), 40

Oregon v. Hass, 420 U.S. 714 (1975), 39

Oregon v. Kennedy, 456 U.S. 667 (1982), 29

Orozco v. Texas, 394 U.S. 324 (1969), 36

Oyler v. Boles, 368 U.S. 448 (1962), 44

Pate v. Robinson, 383 U.S. 375 (1966), 53

Payton v. New York, 445 U.S. 573 (1980), 15

Pennsylvania v. Mimms, 434 U.S. 106 (1977), 24

Pennsylvania v. Muniz, 496 U.S. 582 (1990), 37

Piemonte v. United States, 367 U.S. 556 (1961), 34

Price v. Georgia, 398 U.S. 323 (1970), 30

Rakas v. Illinois, 439 U.S. 128 (1978), 14

Randolph v. Georgia, 547 U.S. 103 (2006), 25

Rawlings v. Kentucky, 448 U.S. 98 (1980), 14

Rhode Island v. Innis, 446 U.S. 291 (1980), 37, 65

Richmond Newspapers, Inc. v. Virginia, 448 U.S. 555 (1980), 47

Rochin v. California, 342 U.S. 165 (1952), 22

Roviaro v. United States, 353 U.S. 53 (1957), 17

Schmerber v. California, 384 U.S. 757 (1966), 22, 33

Schneckloth v. Bustamonte, 412 U.S. 218 (1973), 25

Sheppard v. Maxwell, 384 U.S. 333 (1966), 48

Silverthorn Lumber Co. v. United States, 251 U.S. 385, 40 S.Ct. 182 (1920), 10

South Dakota v. Opperman, 428 U.S. 364 (1976), 27

Spinelli v. United States, 393 U.S. 410 (1969), 17

Steagald v. United States, 451 U.S. 204 (1981), 15

Stovall v. Denno, 388 U.S. 293 (1967), 58

Strickland v. Washington, 466 U.S. 668 (1984), 61

Taylor v. Alabama, 457 U.S. 687 (1982), 13

Taylor v. Louisiana, 419 U.S. 522 (1975), 49

Terry v. Ohio, 392 U.S. 1 (1968), 24, 65

U.S. v. Leon, 468 U.S. 897 (1984), 11

United States v. Agurs, 427 U.S. 97 (1976), 51

United States v. Ash, 413 U.S. 300 (1973), 56, 59, 65

United States v. Bagley, 473 U.S. 667 (1985), 51

United States v. Batchelder, 442 U.S. 114 (1979), 44

United States v. Calandra, 414 U.S. 338 (1974), 11

United States v. Chadwick, 433 U.S. 1 (1977), 20, 21, 65

United States v. Cronic, 466 U.S. 648 (1984), 62

United States v. Dickerson, 530 U.S. 428 (2000), 39, 66

United States v. Dixon, 509 U.S. 688 (1993), 31

United States v. Gouveia, 467 U.S. 180 (1984), 57

United States v. Grubbs, 547 U.S. 90 (2006), 16

United States v. Lovasco, 431 U.S. 783 (1977), 46

United States v. Marion, 404 U.S. 307 (1971), 45

United States v. Mendenhall, 446 U.S. 544 (1980), 24, 25

United States v. Montoya de Hernandez, 473 U.S. 531 (1985), 22, 66

United States v. Patane, 124 S.Ct. 2620 (2004), 38

United States v. Payner, 447 U.S. 727 (1980), 14

United States v. Robinson, 414 U.S. 218 (1973), 20

United States v. Ross, 456 U.S. 798 (1982), 21, 65

United States v. Wade, 388 U.S. 218 (1967), 57, 58, 64

United States v. Ward, 448 U.S. 242 (1980), 34

Waller v. Georgia, 464 U.S. 501 (1984), 47

Ward v. City of Monroeville, 93 S.Ct. 80 (1972), 52

Warden v. Hayden, 387 U.S. 294 (1967), 21, 64

Weeks v. United States, 232 U.S. 383, 34 S.Ct. 341 (1914), 10, 19

Whren v. United States, 517 U.S. 806 (1996), 23

Wilson v. Arkansas, 514 U.S. 927 (1995), 19

Witherspoon v. Illinois, 391 U.S. 510 (1968), 49

Wolf v. People of the State of Colorado, 338 U.S. 25, 69 S.Ct. 1359 (1949), 11

Wong Sun v. United States, 371 U.S. 471 (1963), 12, 13, 64

Yick Wo v. Hopkins, 118 U.S. 356 (1886), 44

THEMATIC INDEX

A

arrest warrants. *See* arrests
arrests
    arrest warrants, 15
    definition, 14
assault, 55

B

bona fide purchaser, 8

C

Carroll Doctrine, 20, 27
Confrontation Clause. *See* Constitution of the United States
Constitution of the United States
    Bill of Rights, 10, 32, 54
    Confrontation Clause, 52, 53, 54, 55, 65, 66
        history, 53
        limitations, 55
    Double Jeopardy Clause, 27, 28, 29, 30, 31, 32
        collateral estoppel, 29
        Dual Sovereignty Doctrine, 31
        retroactivity, 33
    Eighth Amendment, 10
    Equal Protection Clause, 44, 49
    Fifth Amendment, 10, 13, 27, 33, 34, 35, 36, 38, 39, 41, 42, 43, 44, 53, 57, 64
    First Amendment, 46, 47
    Fourteenth Amendment, 10, 11, 22, 28, 44, 46, 48, 49, 50, 59, 60
    Fourth Amendment, 10, 11, 12, 13, 14, 15, 16, 21, 22, 23, 25, 26, 27, 66
    Self-Incrimination Clause, 33
        "Fruit of the Poisonous Tree" Doctrine, 40
        Exclusionary Remedy, 38
        Miranda Safeguards, 35
        Public Safety Exception, 39
        repeat confessions, 40
        right to counsel in interrogations, 40
    Seventh Amendment, 10
    Sixth Amendment, 10, 33, 40, 41, 45, 47, 48, 49, 51, 52, 53, 54, 56, 57, 58, 59, 60, 62, 63, 64, 65
        right to a fair trial, 46, 49, 50, 51
        right to a speedy trial, 45
        right to a trial by an impartial jury, 48
        right to counsel, 56
            conflicts of interest, 62
            right to experts, 60
            self-representation, 63
curtilage, 14, 19

D

Double Jeopardy Clause. *See* Constitution of the United States
due process
    procedural due process
        state action, 34
    substantive due process
        privacy, 13

E

Emergency Doctrine, 21
Exclusionary Rule, 10, 11, 13
    "Fruit of the Poisonous Tree" Doctrine, 12
    applied to the Fifth Amendment, 13
    limitations, 11
excuse
    insanity(mental abnormality), 53, 60

F

false imprisonment, 8
Federal Rules of Evidence, 8, 54, 65
findings, 47
Frisk after Terry Stop, 24

G

Grand Jury, 43, 44, 45

I

inventory search, 26

J

joint and several liability, 8
jurisdiction
    personal jurisdiction, 9
    subject matter jurisdiction, 9
justiciability
    standing, 11, 13, 14
justification, 22

M

Model Penal Code, 8

P

privileges, 33, 34, 35, 42, 55

R

regulatory searches, 26
Religious Freedom Restoration Act of 1993, 9
res ipsa loquitur, 9
Right to a Trial by Jury, 64
Right to Counsel. *See* Constitution of the United States (Sixth Amendment)

S

search incident to lawful arrest, 19
search warrants, 16, 26
    execution, 18
    Four Corners Rule, 18
    probable cause, 16, 17
    requirements of a valid warrant, 16
Self-Incrimination Clause. *See* Constitution of the United States
strict liability, 9

T

takings
    public use, 12

U

Uniform Commercial Code, 9